THE AIRBORNE INVASION OF CRETE

Published by Books Express Publishing
Copyright © Books Express, 2011
ISBN 978-1-78039-065-9

Books Express publications are available from all good retail and online booksellers. For publishing proposals and direct ordering please contact us at: info@books-express.com

AIR-BORNE INVASION OF CRETE

Foreword

This report on the Air-Borne Invasion of Crete is believed to be of such importance to the Armed Forces of the United States that it is reproduced in its entirety and given a wide distribution. It amplifies Special Bulletin No. 35, subject: "The Battle of Crete, May 20 - June 1, 1941", issued October 15, 1941.

Much of the material in this report was gained from persons who were on Crete at the time of the attack. Generally their names have been deleted.

Attention is invited to the classification, "Secret". Its contents must be closely guarded.

SHERMAN MILES,
Brigadier General, U. S. Army,
Acting Assistant Chief of Staff, G-2.

Distribution:	Copy No.
Secretary of War	1
Under Secretary of War	2
Assistant Secretary of War	3
Asst. Secretary of War for Air	4
Secretary General Staff	5
Asst. Chief of Staff, WPD	6
Asst. Chief of Staff, G-1	7
Asst. Chief of Staff, G-2	8 to 17 incl.
Asst. Chief of Staff, G-3	18 to 20 incl.
Asst. Chief of Staff, G-4	21
G.H.Q.	22 to 36 incl.
Air	
(General Arnold	37
(AFCC	38
(ADC	39 to 40 incl.
(Chief of Air Corps	41 to 42 incl.
The Chief of Cavalry	43 to 46 incl.
The Chief of Field Artillery	47 to 50 incl.
The Chief of Infantry	51 to 54 incl.
The Chief of Coast Artillery	55 to 58 incl.
The Chief of Engineers	59 to 62 incl.
The Chief Signal Officer	63 to 66 incl.
The Chief of C.W.S.	67 to 70 incl.
Quartermaster	71 to 72 incl.
Surgeon General	73 to 74 incl.
Chief of Ordnance	75 to 76 incl.
Hq. Caribbean D. C.	77 to 86 incl.
Philippine Department	87 to 91 incl.
Hawaii Department	92 to 96 incl.
Command & General Staff School	97 to 98 incl.
Office of Naval Intelligence	99 to 100 incl.

MID 370.03 Germany 9-8-41

MILITARY INTELLIGENCE DIVISION
WAR DEPARTMENT GENERAL STAFF

MILITARY ATTACHE REPORT: EGYPT.

SUBJECT: AIR-BORNE INVASION OF CRETE.   I. G. No. 9900.

SOURCE AND DEGREE OF RELIABILITY: Attached appendices; personal conversation with numerous participants; conferences with Gen. Freyberg, various members Army and RAF Intelligence Division; official files, Middle East. Sources: Original. Reliable.

SUMMARIZATION OF REPORT. This is a narrative of the Air-borne Invasion of Crete with certain conclusions and recommendations.

INTRODUCTION:

The drama of CRETE marks an epic in warfare. The concept of the operation was highly imaginative, daringly new. Combat elements drawn from Central EUROPE moved with precision into funnel shaped GREECE. Here they re-formed, took shape as a balanced force, were given wings. The operation had the movement, rhythm, harmony of a master's organ composition. On 20 May and succeeding days this force soared through space; its elements broke over CRETE in thundering crescendos -- all stops out. For the first time in history air-borne troops, supplied and supported by air, landed in the face of an enemy, defeated him. For the first time an air force defeated a first-rate Navy, inflicted such staggering losses that the fleet was ordered back to ALEXANDRIA three days after the battle started.

In the spring of 1941 the British forces in Middle East were spread too thin. With inadequate means to justify the expedition, Great Britain made a valiant attempt to carry the war from AFRICA to EUROPE. In GREECE this attempt failed. Lack of sea transport and force of naval circumstances dictated that evacuees from GREECE be taken to CRETE rather than EGYPT.

At CRETE, with time and means limited, defenses were stiffened. But effective preliminary effort and superb hand-to-hand fighting were not enough. CRETE fell because the British had no air power to oppose the German air invasion.

From M.A. Cairo, Egypt. Report No. 1987.   8 September 1941.

In GREECE the RAF strength had been most inadequate. Yet in view of Axis success in CYRENAICA, possibly more aircraft had been sent to GREECE than was justifiable. Few of those planes returned. At the end of April there were 43 fighters and 90 bombers operational in EGYPT and CRETE. Obviously no amount of spade work at CRETE could off-set this hopeless deficiency in air power.

Middle East was aware of the difficulties of defending CRETE. On 28 April, the day of his arrival in CRETE, General Wilson cabled Middle East that unless the three services were prepared to maintain adequate forces, the holding of CRETE was a dangerous commitment. He asked for an immediate decision. The RAF admitted its CRETE air force was impotent and that it would be some time before additional aircraft could be sent. The Navy realized that without fighter support it was madness for them to attempt operations in CRETE waters. General Freyberg reported he would fight but had no hope of being able to repel an invasion without full support of Navy and Air Force. Appreciating Freyberg's position, General Wavell sent all available materiel to CRETE, continued his efforts to secure additional means from GREAT BRITAIN.

Because of the Nazi Air Force the problem of moving evacuees from CRETE was a task the Navy was loathe to undertake. Moreover the Navy wanted CRETE, the key to the AEGEAN, to be made into a second MALTA. CRETE gave Britain air bases from which Roumanian oil could be bombed; from which the CORINTH CANAL, useful to Axis supply, could be controlled; from which RAF fighters could strike Nazi long-range bombers, based on GREECE and DODECANESE, destined for RED SEA service. It gave Britain a toe-hold for anticipated operations on the Continent. The War Ministry was anxious to hold CRETE as a seat for the Greek Government.

Holding CRETE denied the German Air Force bases complementing those to the south in CYRENAICA; it prevented him from freedom of action in the AEGEAN; it precluded use of CRETE airdromes for attacks on British bases in EGYPT and shipping in the RED SEA.

In early May the fleet was engaged in important MEDITERRANEAN convoy duties which precluded its use for evacuation before the attack came. There was no alternative other than to defend CRETE.

An almost unlimited number of airdromes, situated in depth and extending from the DODECANESE through GREECE to SICILY gave the German Air Force dispersion advantage and permitted a three-way converging attack. CRETE is small; rugged terrain restricts its landing areas. Since aircraft based on CRETE could not be widely dispersed, obviously they could not survive a major attack. Due to distance such support from aircraft based in EGYPT as was available proved ineffective. However, given the most advantageously located bases, the entire RAF in Middle East was so depleted that it could have done little more than delay the final capitulation.

From M.A. Cairo, Egypt. Report No. 1987.   8 September 1941.

No one envisaged the intensity of the air atttck which was launched against CRETE. With bomb proofs, ample 25-pounders, AA guns and mechanized units, with the New Zealand Division fresh as it was when it went to GREECE, heavier losses would have been inflicted upon the enemy, but more likely than not the outcome would have been the same. Moreover, so devastatingly effective was the Nazi air force on shipping that CRETE could not have been supplied. Unless Britain could neutralize the German Air Force, loss of CRETE was inevitable. The responsibility must rest on those whose decision it was to carry the war to EUROPE.

PLAN OF ATTACK:

The reason for the German attack on CRETE was not entirely clear until she disclosed her intent toward U.S.S.R. CRETE is the keystone of the island barriers to the AEGEAN. A Nazi AEGEAN lends itself to possible combined operations against TURKEY from the BOSPHORUS and from the west. With German control of the AEGEAN, only the U.S.S.R. is in a position to challenge Axis vessels in the BLACK SEA.

The capture of CRETE was not regarded as a major operation for the German intelligence on 19 May published:

"There are no Greek troops in CRETE. The British troops are a permanent garrison. British troops which fled from the PELOPONESE have been brought to ALEXANDRIA." The Nazi listed British forces on CRETE as "3 battalions of infantry, 30 light tanks, 30 AA guns, 40 AA machine guns, 9 coast defense guns". The German estimate was grossly inaccurate; their losses the first day were so appalling that on the second day of the battle the High Command was forced either to give up or launch a full scale attack. They chose to hurl 35,000 air-borne troops and their whole available air striking force against CRETE.

The German made the most of the twenty odd Greek airdromes which he found available. In addition many landing areas were prepared in the southern part of PELOPONESE. The advantages which forward landing fields offered dive bombers and fighters were exploited to the limit. At times from positions off the northwest coast of CRETE the Royal Navy could see dive bombers take off, proceed to their target, return for more bombs. It was the most rapid, damaging, ghastly air shuttle service imaginable.

Fighters and dive bombers used newly constructed landing fields on the southern PELOPONESE and airdromes at MOLAOI, MILOS, CORINTH, ARGOS, SCARPANTO. Transport planes came generally from the ATHENS-CORINTH area; some came from SEDES and MIKRA airports at SALONIKA. Long-range bombers took off from airdromes in the vicinity of THEBES and SALONIKA. Italian bombers from RHODES and German bombers from SICILY operated against shipping.

From M.A. Cairo, Egypt. Report No. 1987.   8 September 1941.

The mission assigned Fliegerkorps XI was to capture the island of CRETE and hold until relieved by the Army. Fliegerkorps XI, which controlled the operation, had under its command the parachute and glider troops of Fliegerdivisions VII. Also attached were the 22nd Air-borne Division, the 5th and 6th Mountain Divisions, the fighters and bombers of Fliegerkorps VIII.

It was intended for the air-borne forces to capture CRETE, then to be relieved by the sea-borne 5th Mountain Division which was to garrison the island. As the attack developed the defenses proved stronger than was expected. Effective fleet action disrupted two sea-borne expeditions. Consequently it became necessary for Fliegerkorps XI to send the greater portion of the 5th Mountain Division and two regiments of the 6th Mountain Division to CRETE by air.

During the first few days of the attack 35,000 troops fully equipped for battle were flown into CRETE (X). For the initial attack this force was divided into three groups:

Western - Storm Regiment, reinforced; objective MALEME airdrome.

Central - 7th Air Division (less 1st Parachute Regiment and 2nd Battalion of 2nd Parachute Regiment), 100th Mountain Regiment, two companies Storm Regiments, Parachute Battalions of Pioneers, AA, Machine Gun and a Medical Company, objective for first wave CANEA, for second wave RETIMO.

Eastern - 1st Parachute Regiment, 85th Alpine Regiment; objective HERAKLION. (Map 1)

These initial attacking forces were about 15,500 strong, with 799 light machine guns, 48 anti-tank guns, 81 mortars, 37 75-millimeter cannon.

The War Office appreciation of 29 April to General Freyberg must have stunned him. Based on most reliable sources it claimed a simultaneous air and sea-borne attack was imminent. The estimate reckoned three to four thousand air-borne troops in the first sortie, two or three sorties per day from GREECE, three or four from RHODES. All sorties would have fighter protection. Preceding troop invasions heavy bombing and machine gun preparations on troops could be expected. There were available for the operation 315 long-range bombers, 240

(X) The troops flown into CRETE were as follows:

5th Mountain Division, 9000; 6th Mountain Division, 7000; Fliegerkorps VII - Storm Regiment glider troops, 1000 - 1st, 2nd, 3rd Parachute Regiments, 5400 - Special Troops - Machine Gun Bn., AA Machine Gun Bn., Motorcycle Bn., Engineer Bn., Medical Company, Anti-tank Unit, Battery of Artillery, 3600; 22nd Air-borne Division - 16th, 47th, 65th Regiments, 9000. Total 35,000.

From M.A. Cairo, Egypt. Report No. 1987.   8 September 1941.

dive bombers, 60 twin motor fighters, 270 single-motor fighters, 40 reconnaissance planes. General Freyberg estimates 1,200 transport planes were used. Since attack developed into an all-out performance, doubtless all available aircraft were used.

The scale of the sea-borne attack which General Freyberg must meet would depend on ability to evade British Navy.

PROBLEM OF DEFENSE:

General Freyberg disposed his troops in four self-contained groups, one each at MALEME, SUDA BAY, RETIMO, HERAKLION (X). Force Headquarters was near CANEA. One Battalion, Welch Regiment, two depleted British Battalions constituted the reserve.

Defending troops had 49 pieces of captured Italian field artillery - some without instruments, some without sights, each with only three or four hundred rounds of ammunition - ten 3.7 inch, fourteen 3-inch AA guns, 34 Bofors, a few AA machine guns and Pom Poms, twenty-four 36-inch searchlights. There were also eight Infantry tanks, 16 light tanks, a few troop carriers. Most of the Australian and New Zealand Infantry Battalions arrived in CRETE with their rifles, Bren guns, anti-tank rifles, machine guns. There was no other equipment. Few of the men had overcoats. None had bedding. Most had lost their toilet kits. There were no mess facilities.

CRETE forces were divided into three components: 3500 of the original garrison of the 14th Infantry Brigade, with attached naval, artillery, infantry units; evacuees from GREECE of British, Australian, New Zealand units totaling 14,000; 10,000 Palestinians, Cypriots, odds and ends of British units who had lost their organizations. Only the original garrison and the infantry of the Australian, New Zealand and British units were fit for combat. All others had lost their weapons or their units and were not trained in infantry minor tactics.

(X) Disposition by units:

MALEME Sector: H.Q., N.Z. Div. with 2 Brigs. and 1 improvised Brig. including 3 Gk. Bns.; 2 "I" tanks and 10 light tanks; Artillery - 10 captured Italian 75 mm. guns, 6 Howitzers, AA and C.D. artillery. (Map 2, Photo 2)
SUDA BAY: Mobile Naval Base Defense Organization with AA and C.D. artillery and 1 Bn. Royal Marines; 3 British Bns. (depleted), 2 Gk. Bns.; Reinforced by arrival of "Layforce" - Commandos - toward end of battle. (Maps 2, 3, 6; Photo 3)
RETIMO: 4 Aust. Inf. Bns. (2 Bns. moved to CANEA Sector during battle); 2 "I" tanks; C.D. and captured field artillery. (Map 4A, Photo 3)
HERAKLION: 14 Inf. Brig. (British); 4 Gk. Bns.; 2/4 Aust. Inf. Bn., 7 Medium Regt. R.A. (less one bty Rifle Bn.); 2 "I" tanks and 6 light tanks; AA and C.D. and captured field artillery; Reinforced by Argyle and Sutherland Highlanders from EGYPT during battle; also 2 "I" tanks. (Map 4, Photo 5)

From M.A. Cairo, Egypt. Report No. 1987.   8 September 1941.

It is easy now to criticize the British for not using local material and labor to prepare better defensive positions. But no material for construction was available. Steel and concrete for pill boxes were not available. There were few shovels, little transport. Not only were CRETE supplies depleted but also its young and vigorous man power had been taken to GREECE during the Greek-Italian war.

There is criticism that the road net from south to north was not developed so that southern ports, which required less daylight exposure of incoming and outgoing vessels than northern ports, might be used. However, it was only a few minutes further by air to the southern ports and any active harbor there would have received the same treatment accorded SUDA BAY.

But had the road net been perfect, had southern ports been used exclusively, it would not have solved the supply problem. Waters about CRETE were untenable. CRETE'S supply line was vulnerable to air attack all the way to EGYPT. On the open sea the Nazi air attack on shipping was vicious; some ships were sunk, others were set on fire.

The only way ships could unload at SUDA docks was to enter after dark and leave before daylight. Only destroyers were fast enough to slip in and out with any degree of safety. They arrived at 11:30 p.m.; were compelled to leave at 3:00 in the morning. Maximum accommodation was two vessels and by fast work 100 tons could be unloaded during this period. For days no ships at all arrived. Since the forces required six hundred tons per day heavy inroads had to be made on the reserves.

Out of 100 field pieces sent from Middle East only 49 arrived. In an attempt to create a twenty-day reserve stock for 20,000 troops, 21,000 tons were transported to CRETE but sent back because they could not be unloaded; 2,700 tons were unloaded; 3,400 tons were sunk. Since CRETE'S normal population of 440,000 had been augmented by 14,000 Greek soldiers, 15,000 Italian prisoners and 27,550 British troops, obviously CRETE could not have been supplied under existing air conditions.

Lack of roads, location of landing fields and possible landing beaches complicated the defense. Machine gun and bombing attacks from the air and vertical envelopment by air-borne troops offered the defender slight opportunity to take advantage of terrain. Since air attacks made movement by day impossible, concealment became more important than position. Because there were very few suitable landing grounds it was possible to defend all of them. Consequently air-borne troops were compelled to land in defended areas. Air photographs, constant reconnaissance, retention of the initiative, gave the Nazi every other advantage.

In spite of the fact that they were inadequately equipped, without air support, their supply, reinforcement, evacuation problems unsolved, most of the troops were in good spirits. Although they had already had enough in GREECE, the war-weary troops steeled themselves

From M.A. Cairo, Egypt. Report No. 1987.   8 September 1941.

for the first Air Army invasion in history. In so far as individual performance against great odds goes, no forces ever gave better account.

PRELUDE TO AIR ARMY ATTACK:

A month prior to the main attack there had been a general movement south. Transport planes, gliders, gathered in the region of ATHENS and CORINTH; special troops came by air, sea, road, rail. Supplies and enormous stocks of munitions were piled well forward (X). Landing fields were hastily constructed in Southern GREECE; AEGEAN Islands offering landing facilities were seized. At MILOS British officers and men were captured, put to work constructing landing grounds.

There were three phases to the preparation prior to the attack by air-borne troops.

The first ten days of May was a period of thorough reconnaissance accompanied by light dive bombing and machine gun attacks. The Nazi plan for the main attack was based on the extensive series of air photographs taken at this time.

In the second phase daylight bombings and machine gun attacks of increasing scale, frequency, and intensity began. Vicious thrusts at communications, probing attacks to locate AA, troop concentrations, defensive positions, were launched. Fighters struck the few remaining RAF planes, forced a decision on the 15th to withdraw all aircraft to EGYPT.

The third phase was a series of fierce attacks against sea communications to interrupt supplies. One night, operating singly, planes bombed SUDA BAY continuously for seven hours. On the 17th seventeen JU 88's, escorted by ten ME 109's, dive bombed SUDA BAY. The day following, after four reconnaissances, SUDA BAY caught seven heavy attacks supported by fighters. Unloading was continued while ships were on fire and sinking. SUDA anchorage became a graveyard for vessels. (Map 6 and Photo 1) On MALEME and HERAKLION airdromes bombing and machine gun attacks were heavy and frequent. There was a general intensification of all attacks to break down morale.

Throughout the month preceding 20 May there was a constantly rising tempo in the preparation for the air-borne invasion. The method of attacks varied; their intensity progressively increased. Daily reconnaissance and air photography enabled the Nazi to study defense disposition of troops, location of guns, slit trenches. Having completed thorough reconnaissance, having beaten down resistance, having interrupted supply, the Nazi air army was ready to attack.

(X)   When the British evacuated GREECE they left 67,000 tons of gasoline at PIRAEUS.

From M.A. Cairo, Egypt. Report No. 1987.   8 September 1941.

AIR ARMY ATTACK:

Soon after dawn 20 May the Luftwaffe struck the MALEME-CANEA area. The objective was to silence AA batteries and to prevent use of the roads between SUDA and MALEME. At MALEME the attack was especially heavy.

The New Zealand 22nd Battalion guarding MALEME airdrome was heavily bombarded and machine gunned for ninety minutes by JU 87's, JU 88's, ME 109's, ME 110's. The intensity was so terrific that everyone was driven to slit trenches; some participants claim the severity of the attack exceeded the heaviest artillery preparations of the World War. Before the dense cloud resulting from this attack lifted, fifty gliders had landed in the dry river bed directly in front and to the west of the 22nd Battalion. (Map 2)

The big scale BLITZ was an awful spectacle. General Freyberg relates how he stood on a hill watching the attack over MALEME enthralled by the magnitude of the operation. While he was watching the bombers he suddenly became aware of a greater throbbing, or overtone, during the moments of comparative quiet. Looking to sea he saw hundreds of planes, tier upon tier, coming toward him. They were huge, slow-moving troop carriers with the air-borne troops he had been expecting. They circled counter clock-wise over MALEME airdrome and then, only 200 feet above the ground, as if by magic white specks suddenly appeared beneath the planes. Colored clouds of parachutists floated slowly to earth.

The dry stream banks afforded shelter to the glider-borne troops who landed there. Fully armed and organized as combat teams, troops poured out of gliders, took up positions facing the 22nd Battalion. Flying at low altitude in circles whose center was about a half mile west of the 22nd Battalion position, Nazi fighters covered the descent of the parachutists by continuous murderous straffing of ground troops. (Map 2)

Most of the parachutists who landed near defending troops were killed. Some who landed on the MALEME-CANEA road interrupted communications. On the airdrome defending troops were overwhelmed by parachutists who, with stores and equipment, actually landed on top of them. To the east and west of the airdrome JU 52's crashlanded on the beaches, disgorged troops. The eastern group threatened the rear of the 22nd Battalion; the western group joined those in the wadi. The wadi troops formed the nucleus of the forces which eventually captured the island.

The day of bitter fighting was replete with intense bombardments and straffing. The New Zealanders made eight successful bayonet charges; murderous air attacks forced them to relinquish their gains. During the night, the 22nd Battalion withdrew a half mile to the east. MALEME airdrome, however, was still held under artillery and machine gun fire.

From M. A. Cairo, Egypt. Report No. 1987.   8 September 1941.

Simultaneously with the MALEME airdrome attack, 1800 glider-borne and parachute troops had landed southwest of CANEA near the 4th New Zealand Brigade. A Ranger Company and the Royal Perivolians, with Bren carriers mopped up all parachutists except those in the prison of AGHYA area. At the close of a day of heavy fighting the 4th Brigade held its position. (Map 2 and Photo 4)

On the AKROTIRI Peninsula eleven gliders landed soon after dawn. These troops, as well as those who landed about SUDA BAY, attacked AA gun crews. Few gunners had rifles; their losses were heavy. The Northumberland Hussars and a Ranger Company, who were defending the peninsula, promptly wiped out all glider troops except some who took cover in an abandoned gun position.

Throughout the day at RETIMO there was spasmodic bombing and straffing. At 1600 hours one hundred seventy troop carriers appeared; 1,700 parachutists floated to earth, landed about the airdrome, on the high ground to the southeast. Most of them were killed but those on the high ground captured some field pieces, two infantry tanks, held their position. A small group of parachutists landed at the road fork between RETIMO and the AIRDROME, blocked the road, cut the communications. Fighting continued throughout the night. (Map 4A)

During intermittent air activity HERAKLION defended itself remarkably well. Simultaneously with the RETIMO parachute attack two hundred troop carriers appeared from the north in two great waves; two thousand parachutists were dropped west and south of the town and about the airdrome. All who landed within the perimeter were killed. (Map 4)

In the first day of attack the 22nd New Zealand Battalion was forced from MALEME airdrome; the airdrome remained under fire; SUDA BAY area, RETIMO, HERAKLION still held; all communications were badly interrupted; British believed they had destroyed eighty per cent of the parachutists.

Wednesday 21st - Day 2 - Artillery fire from captured Italian pieces destroyed numbers of planes as they landed on MALEME airdrome, several crash-landed on the nearby beaches. Those wrecked were dragged off the landing ground to make room for more. It is estimated that 600 transports landed during the day. Motorcycles, guns, troop carriers were landed. The Nazi took heavy losses. Dive bombers struck back at the artillery which covered the airdrome, put them out of action. At 1615 hours five hundred parachutists landed behind airdrome defenses, rendered the MALEME position still more precarious. (Photo 2)

From AGHYA prison area a three-hour German attack on GALATOS was repulsed. Invaders about SUDA BAY were well mopped up; all day the situation was completely in hand.

The RETIMO forces counter-attacked, retook their field guns and tanks, cleared the airdrome of parachutists. Parachute forces which remained on either side of the airdrome were reinforced. By

From M.A. Cairo, Egypt. Report No. 1987.   8 September 1941.

cutting communications from RETIMO to HERAKLION and CANEA these forces played a vital part in the ultimate fate of the RETIMO troops.

After a day of bitter fighting HERAKLION town and airdrome remained in the hands of the British. (Photo 5)

At the close of the second day of the attack only MALEME seemed insecure; disrupted by the Navy, the Nazi sea-borne invasion had failed.

Thursday 22nd - Day 3 - At dawn two battalions of the New Zealand Division attacked with bayonets, reached MALEME airdrome. The fierceness of the fighting was not surpassed by anything the participating officers had seen at GALLIPOLI or in FRANCE in the first World War. But during daylight no troops could hold the airdrome. Under the murderous fire power which four hundred unopposed fighters delivered, troops were dive bombed and machine gunned off the airdrome, driven back, held in cover positions.

During this morning there was a slight lull in CRETE bombing while the Luftwaffe struck and decisively defeated the fleet in the KYTHERA CHANNEL. Losses were so heavy the battle may some day be known as Britain's greatest naval disaster.

Throughout the entire day air-borne troops poured in, quickly building fresh formidable forces.

Although the troops had counter-attacked with the bayonet some twenty times, General Freyberg determined to reinforce his 4th Brigade, make one last desperate attack for the airdrome. But before the counter-attack could be launched, from the vicinity of AGHYA prison, the Nazi drove a wedge between the 4th Brigade southwest of CANEA and the 5th Brigade at MALEME. The MALEME garrison was in danger of being cut off; counter-attack had to be abandoned.

At the close of the third day HERAKLION and RETIMO could control their respective areas provided their enemy was not reinforced. The threat to rear of the MALEME troops forced them to seek security by establishing a northwest-southwest line through GALATOS. MALEME became an enemy operational airdrome only eleven miles from SUDA BAY. Freyberg cabled Wavell situation at MALEME very critical, to send all available AIR help.

Friday 23rd - Day 4 - The final part of the withdrawal of the 5th Brigade had to be made during daylight; it was tough fighting to reach the GALATOS line. Fortunately the German air forces were occupied on the roads between CANEA and SUDA and on CANEA itself and the withdrawing units escaped air attack. Air-borne troops continued to arrive; the New Zealand forces had lost half their strength. It was clear the German objective was SUDA BAY.

Throughout the 23rd RETIMO held. Bombing was heavy; there were many British and German wounded; medical supplies were insufficient.

From M.A. Cairo, Egypt. Report No. 1987.   8 September 1941.

heavily bombed, held. The supply situation was causing anxiety. Ammunition and medical stores were desperately needed. Acute ration shortage forced a thirty per cent cut. On this day Churchill cabled Freyberg that great things turned on the splendid CRETE battle which the whole world watched. However splendid the battle appeared in the eyes of the world, Freyberg knew CRETE was lost.

Saturday 24th - Day 5 - The German intensified his air attacks, strengthened his forces with fresh, newly arrived air-borne troops, prepared to attack the New Zealand position. All British troops were very tired. Fighting had been savage; man to man British forces were superior. But unfortunately this was not a man-to-man battle. Air support gave the German tremendous advantage.

Sunday 25th - Day 6 - The night of 24/25 May part of the Layforce - a Commando group commanded by Brigadier Laycock - arrived by destroyer at SUDA BAY. It had been intended to use the Layforce for a landing behind the enemy position but the situation had deteriorated so badly that it had to be used as a rear guard. Vicious bombing, straffing, arrival of heavy reinforcements, pressure from German ground troops made it clear that the men could not hold out much longer.

At eight in the evening the German broke through the New Zealand position, captured GALATOS; the tired 18th and 20th Battalions counter-attacked with the bayonet, retook the village. General Freyberg rates this bayonet attack one of the great efforts of the CRETE defense. It is reported the Germans have erected a joint German-New Zealand memorial at GALATOS.

At HERAKLION the situation was unaltered. Part of the Argyle and Sutherland Highlanders had arrived from TYMBAKI. The German was amassing his troops for an attack. RETIMO, heavily bombed throughout the day, was holding.

Monday 26th - Day 7 - There was bitter fighting all day in SUDA area; bombing and machine gunning were continuous. Bombers lashed unmercifully at SUDA base. All telephone lines were destroyed; communication was possible only by runner.

The Force Reserve, consisting of the Northumberland Hussars, Welch and Ranger Regiments, was on the neck of the AKROTIRI Peninsula between SUDA and CANEA. Southwest of CANEA the depleted New Zealand Division and other units were hard pressed. From the front troops were pouring back toward SUDA. (Map 3).

In a desperate attempt to stabilize the situation General Freyberg ordered his Force Reserve to move forward at midnight and relieve the pressure on the New Zealand Division. At all costs the base at SUDA had to be covered so that essential supplies and reinforcements due by destroyer that night might be unloaded. By late afternoon, however, the New Zealand position deteriorated rapidly. It was necessary to withdraw.

Every effort was made to inform Force Reserve of the withdrawal but the message could not be delivered. At midnight Force Reserve went forward to CANEA-MALEME road not knowing the New Zealand Division had withdrawn.

From M.A. Cairo, Egypt. Report No. 1987.   8 September 1941.

During the day German pressure from the west increased materially, air attacks intensified. On SUDA BAY no vessel could remain afloat; except at night no troop movement was possible. Although withdrawal to the south would force units off their supply line, there remained no other alternative. This day the War Office cabled Freyberg that his glorious battle commanded admiration in all lands; that the enemy was hard pressed; that all aid in "our power" was being sent.

Tuesday 27th - Day 8 - At dawn the Welch Regiment was in position a mile west of CANEA. Patrols were sent out to the west and south; none returned. What had happened was the bulk of the British forces had withdrawn to 42ND STREET and the Welch Regiment had marched into enemy territory. On the AKROTIRI Peninsula, parachutists and caique-borne troops moved south, covered the CANEA-SUDA road with mortars. (Map 3)

During this afternoon orders to evacuate were received. The forces at RETIMO had fought exceptionally well. The escaped prisoners from CRETE have since revealed that up until the 27th their garrison reckoned it had won its battle. RETIMO was completely cut off from General Freyberg's Headquarters. A messenger attempted to reach RETIMO by boat and a plane was sent from Middle East. Both failed to deliver the word to evacuate. Most of the RETIMO garrison was forced to surrender; some escaped to the hills eventually made their way to EGYPT. At HERAKLION the German strengthened his position and reinforced heavily.

Wednesday 28th - Day 9 - During the night of 27/28 the 5th New Zealand and the 19th Australian Brigades withdrew to STILOS where they were heavily attacked. Two Commando groups under Brigadier Laycock, which occupied a position east of SUDA, formed the rear guard for the withdrawal.

At HERAKLION two more battalions of parachute troops and materiel were dropped. HERAKLION forces received orders from Middle East that the Navy would evacuate them the night of the 28th. At ten o'clock embarkation commenced. At 3:00 a.m. the ORION, PHOEBE, PERTH and IMPERIAL moved out with the entire force. The loading had been uneventful. But all day the 30th the convoy was dive bombed. The ORION received three direct hits from 1000-pound bombs. Over four hundred were killed, the force of the explosion imprisoned many; it was days before the bodies could be removed from the ship. The other ships were dive bombed with varying degrees of damage. From the start of the attack until the vessels arrived in ALEXANDRIA the troops never saw an RAF plane.

On the 29th from his Headquarters at SPHAKIA General Freyberg reported to Middle East that the strength of units still capable of organized resistance in the withdrawal was less than 2,000. They had 140 rounds of artillery ammunition and three light tanks.

A thousand troops were evacuated from SPHAKIA the 28/29 May; the night of 29/30 seven thousand were evacuated. On the 30/31 two destroyers and two Sunderlands took off 1,400. (Map 5)

From M.A. Cairo, Egypt. Report No. 1987. 8 September 1941.

Fighting troops had first priority and a fair apportionment among British, Australian, and New Zealand troops had been worked out for the evacuation. Although some Palestinians and Cypriots were out of control enroute SPHAKIA, considering the difficulties, the withdrawal and evacuation were both well executed. Unfortunately not all could be embarked (**X**). The last load was taken out the night 31 May - 1 June. The senior officer remaining behind was instructed to surrender on the morning following.

During the evacuation operation the German air force action was greatly reduced. Had the attack tempo of MALEME continued possibly no one would have escaped. While it was not known at the time, the Nazi air force had a yet heavier assignment: to move north and in three weeks to strike the Red Army.

NAVY:

Before the Greek invasion Admiral Cunningham made his daring and successful sweeps through the MEDITERRANEAN in complete disregard of the Italian air force. When Italian fliers did attack, the fleet put up an AA barrage; the Italians took avoiding action. The fleet was lulled into a false sense of security by the mediocrity of these air attacks.

But over CRETE waters German pilots came out of the sun in steep power dives, utterly disregarded AA fire, released their bombs close over the target. At KYTHERA Straits dive bombing was accompanied by high level bombing and torpedo attacks. Often the bombs struck before the bomber was seen. The fleet AA could only fire barrages into the sun, hope for hits.

The operations about CRETE not only demonstrated the complete inability of a fleet to operate without fighter support in waters over which the enemy had air superiority, but it disclosed the ineffectiveness of Naval AA. Shadows on the screen of the magical R.D.F. gave ample warning of the approach of aircraft. Yet throughout the action our American Naval Observer had knowledge of only two planes shot down (My cable No. 1950. B.F.F.); our American war correspondent on the VALIANT off KYTHERA Straits saw only seven shot down (Appendix 1, page 5). In some cases of major damage or sinking the air attack had been of such intensity and duration and the naval barrages put up had been so wasteful and ineffective that the vessels were out of ammunition long before the bombing ceased.

The German Air Force paralyzed naval operations. Supply delivery was insufficient for continued support of the garrisons; many of the necessary reinforcements from ALEXANDRIA had to turn back or were sunk; evacuation from SUDA BAY was impossible. Evacuation from HERAKLION was costly; from SPHAKIA part of the garrison was evacuated in the dead of night.

In addition to maintenance of sea communications the mission of the Royal Navy was to protect all sea flanks about CRETE.

(**X**) Note: The Navy was justified in abandoning further evacuation. I am reliably informed that on 1 June only 4 destroyers and the QUEEN ELIZABETH remained seaworthy. B.F.F.

From M. A. Cairo, Egypt. Report No. 1987.   8 September 1941.

The night of 21/22 May, the Royal Navy break up a sea-borne expedition enroute from GREECE to CRETE. Twelve caiques and two small steamers were sunk. There were many casualties in other caiques which the Navy attacked off the north coast. Elements of the 5th Mountain Division, detachments of parachute AA, anti-tank, artillery, and machine gun units were lost. The night of 22/23 May the KELLY and the KASHMIR sank many caiques full of soldiers and munitions. This sea-borne expedition, after suffering heavy losses, turned back to MILOS. So far as is now known only one caique load of German troops landed prior to 28 May. On this date, however, the Nazi landed sea-borne troops and tanks and the Italian landed troops at SITEIA BAY. (Map 1)

But the fleet paid dearly for its success in breaking up the sea-borne expeditions. On the morning of 22 May in the Straits of KYTHERA the entire battle fleet was attacked by high level and dive bombers, torpedo and mine dropping aircraft. At one time during the engagement 320 planes were attacking. Two cruisers, at least three destroyers were sunk, all vessels badly damaged. A 2000-pound bomb fell ten feet off the super dreadnaught VALIANT'S port bow, "holing the ship very badly beneath the water line and literally picking her bows out of the water and shifting her course by more than ninety degrees". (Appendix 1, Page 3) It was the first engagement of a first-rate fleet without air support with a first-rate air power. The battle ended in a complete and undeniable air victory.

Deeply concerned Churchill cabled Wavell on the 26th that a CRETE victory was essential, to keep hurling in all aid. Wavell replied: "Reinforcements have steadily become more difficult on account increasing enemy air attacks and may now be considered impossible".

During these operations the Navy considered all CRETE missions madness. There were instances when Commanders demanded fighter escort before they proceeded to CRETE. Such planes as the RAF was able to provide however, due possibly to lack of training, were often unable to locate the ships they were assigned to escort. With their gasoline supply limited they were forced to return to EGYPT. There was never greater need for long-range fighters.

So far as heroism is concerned possibly there are no more valiant deeds in British history than those of the Navy in attempting to supply, defend and evacuate CRETE. But the fact that in eight days the Nazi attack drove the Navy to EGYPT, forced an evacuation which left more than half the garrisons behind, testifies to the total inability of a Navy to operate in waters over which the enemy controls the air.

Note: No official reports of CRETE naval operations were ever made available, although my request for them was pressed as far as it could tactfully be done. I have complete confidence in the data submitted in Appendix 1, pages 1 to 6. The damage inflicted on the ships which remained afloat may still be seen. I personally saw the signal ordering the fleet back to ALEXANDRIA 23 May 1941. B.F.F.

From M.A. Cairo, Egypt. Report No. 1987.   8 September 1941.

ROYAL AIR FORCE:

During the period General Freyberg was preparing CRETE for attack the RAF shot down twenty-three aircraft confirmed and possibly another nine. Many others were damaged. Due to the great numerical superiority of the enemy, by 19 May the RAF on CRETE was reduced to three Hurricanes and three Gladiators. No replacements being available for Middle East, these planes were returned to EGYPT the day before the attack.

On 23 May, however, being desperate for air support and possibly as a gesture, two flights of six Hurricanes each were sent to CRETE from EGYPT. The first flight flew over the Royal Navy whose gunners, being justifiably afflicted with "windiness", put up an unusually effective barrage, shot down two Hurricanes; three returned to EGYPT, one reached HERAKLION. The second flight sustained damage in landing so that out of the twelve planes dispatched only two were serviceable. On 24 May one of the two remaining Hurricanes was burned on the ground.

During the campaign the RAF made many night sorties from EGYPT on military targets in GREECE and CRETE. But the Nazi had phased his CRETE attack in the dark of the moon so that the RAF retaliatory night attacks against enemy airdromes was relatively non-effective. Although losses were inflicted there is nothing to indicate they had the slightest influence on the outcome of the operation.

ANTI-AIRCRAFT:

Because the German attack was successful one is likely to gather the impression that little AA fire had to be silenced. About the two by six mile horse-shoe shaped SUDA BAY the British placed four batteries, each with four 3.7-inch AA guns; five sections each with two 3-inch AA guns; 16 Bofors; two 50-caliber four barrel machine guns and a number of .303-caliber machine guns (Map 1A). In spite of this impressive air defense SUDA BAY was untenable for vessels. At MALEME airdrome two 3-inch AA guns, 10 Bofors, were put out of action quickly on the 20th. At HERAKLION airdrome were four 3-inch AA guns, 10 Bofors, 2 Pom Poms. Each airdrome had about forty machine guns. RETIMO had no AA protection except machine guns.

No complete data is available showing the losses AA guns inflicted. Lieutenant Hughes, who commanded the Bofors at SUDA BAY, reports hits were numerous. But reading of reports available discloses only a few planes were shot down. On 10 May a Bofors shot down two bombers at HERAKLION. On the 16th AA at HERAKLION shot down three aircraft and destroyed three others. AA fire on the 17th drove off thirty ME 109's from MALEME airdrome and shot down one DO 17. The 18th AA shot down one plane. On the 20th at HERAKLION AA shot down sixteen out of 130 troop carriers. Due to extraordinary battle confusion no list of planes shot down after the 20th exists.

From M.A. Cairo, Egypt. Report No. 1987.   8 September 1941.

TECHNIQUE AIR:

Before the air-borne attack the German Air Force objective was reconnaissance, liquidation of AA guns, crews, aircraft. For the air-borne attack the objectives were AA guns, airdromes, vessels, communications, supply dumps. The air force also gave close support to their attacking units. Transports and gliders placed troops tactically.

Before the attack instructions to troops were clear cut, pictured their objective in detail. Preliminary reconnaissance of the objectives was thorough. Every unit commander was required to know his objective from map study, air photographs, sketches. Non-commissioned officers were required to make their own pencil sketch of their objective.

After the initial attack which started at dawn, Nazi airmen did little between the hours of 8 p.m. and 8 a.m. Daily at dawn a low altitude reconnaissance was made to note changes in dispositions of defending troops and guns. As soon as this information was imparted to fighter and dive bomber aircraft the attack began. But reconnaissance continued throughout the day. After an air attack had died down, the slightest ground movement brought back almost immediately a murderous ground straffing.

Communications between ground and air were effective at all times. After their initial landing air-borne troops directed aircraft to specific targets by panel, pyrotechnics. On CRETE wireless was used at all points for ground to ground messages. Ground stations worked German ground Headquarters in CRETE; CRETE Headquarters worked Headquarters Fliegerkorps XI, GREECE. Fliegerkorps XI communicated with aircraft in flight. All messages went in the clear but four hours were added to time and code names were used for things and places.

On the other hand the three garrisons which the British established at CRETE soon had their communications interrupted by parachutists, dive bombers, ground straffers. In forward areas double lines and laddering to provide for breaks did not insure communications.

An airdrome attack began with neutralization of its defending AA. From two or three directions fighters often dived simultaneously and lower than 1,000 feet on AA gun crews. The crew was able to engage one target, not two or three. Consequently they fired a few shots, took cover. Two fighter attacks were usually made on an airdrome. In the first attack the planes were shot full of holes, the gasoline allowed to spread; the second attack usually started fires. Once low over MALEME airdrome airmen staged daring acrobatics so as to draw men out of slit trenches to watch the show. As the men were watching ME 109's suddenly arrived, machine gunned spectators before they could dive in the trenches. Machine gunning was more effective against troops than bombing.

In dive bombing AA positions, planes at 10,000 feet appeared, circled, selected their target, went into steep, sometimes almost vertical dives. At about 3,000 feet they released the bomb, then turned slightly, pulled out, disappeared flying at sea level and at right angles to their dive. Stukas dived with machine guns in action.

From M.A. Cairo, Egypt. Report No. 1987.   8 September 1941.

High level bombing against naval targets by JU 83's was unusually accurate. Planes operated singly or in very loose formation. Occasionally a JU 88 flew around and around the fleet to draw fire, then JU 87's followed with dive bombing. Dive bombers came directly out of the sun, dropped their bombs, pulled back into the sun again. Approaching vessels aft, planes frequently dived in threes; at the beginning of the dive planes were widely separated. Their traces converged on the target. To give the vessel hard right or left rudder was futile for in either case one of the planes was diving directly into the ship longitudinally.

Gliders were directed primarily against heavy AA gun positions. The sketch opposite is a copy of an original taken from a captured glider pilot. Only five companies of fifteen gliders each were used. Three companies were scheduled to land in the wadi west of MALEME, one company on the AKROTIRI Peninsula, one company on the heavy AA positions about SUDA BAY. Gliders were never used after the first fifteen minutes of the attack.

Air bombardments of great intensity preceded glider landing. While heads were down in slit trenches the gliders arrived. Parachutists followed the gliders at a very short interval. Gliders were released at high altitude, came in with air escort, placed combat teams tactically.

In the forward part of the glider ammunition was carried. Machine gun fire from the ground occasionally was effective in exploding this ammunition. After landing the troop passengers, who had been helpless in the air, became immediately a formidable combat team.

One glider company landed in CANEA area had a whole flight of Stukas, twelve ME 109's and six ME 110's scheduled to support it. Stukas bombed AA artillery; the ME's neutralized AA and ground troops. Coordination of glider-borne troops on the ground with air force appeared to be perfect. In spite of the perfection of this particular glider-borne attack, the British defending troops succeeded in destroying the unit.

The JU 52 transport planes flew in "V" formation, carried twelve to fifteen parachutists per plane. Four JU 52's transported a platoon. Troops jumped first, then the ammunition canisters were tossed overboard. Each air-borne trooper carried food and ammunition for two days. Ground troops requisitioned food, ammunition, medical supplies by panel and verey signal. Air deliveries were prompt. Low flying fighters protected the transport freighters.

Air-borne troops supplied and supported by air offered a new and baffling problem to the defenders. Troops were free from the restrictions inherent in ground movement, supply and reinforcement. The attacker of CRETE offered no supply line to be severed, no reserve to be cut off; supplies and reserves came in via vertical supply line which only air power can sever. Reinforcements were never tired from marching, were landed exactly where and when needed fresh for combat. But the Luftwaffe offered still more assistance. After it had transported, supplied, and reinforced units dive bombers and fighters prepared the way for them to move forward, silenced defending artillery, interrupted communication, denied maneuver to the defender during daylight.

From M.A. Cairo, Egypt. Report No. 1987.   8 September 1941.

The CRETE defenses were laid out with the view to using the airdromes and denying their use to the enemy. General Freyberg's dispositions were so well selected that to reach their objectives promptly parachutists were forced to land near his troops. The British had no trouble in destroying most of these parachutists but the delay caused by disposing of them enabled other troops to land upon the defended areas. The defenders' problem, therefore, became one involving movement into a position to attack the troops which were forming outside his defended area. The complete domination of the air by fighters and dive bombers precluded such movement. Being tied to the ground by fire power from the air the British could only move by night. Night operations became habitual and these had to be completed in time to dig in again before dawn.

Among the officers I spoke to there is the feeling that for the CRETE operation the RAF role of bombing strategic targets by night was of little importance. Although well aware that fighter aircraft operations over CRETE would be almost negligible, recent experience taught them the necessity for close air support for the Army. They endorse the attack of strategic objectives but believe no matter how effective, it is no answer to the German air-army cooperation which was so brilliantly demonstrated in GREECE and CRETE. Shortage of aircraft most certainly dictated RAF tactics. They had no fighter and dive bomber aircraft; they had lost their air bases within fighter range of the enemy; they had no long-range fighters capable of operating from Egyptian airdromes.

Strategic bombing by the RAF possibly at the expense of close support of troops dealt a blow to the morale of the Army. Very few soldiers who fought at CRETE saw the RAF in the role of close support. Day after day British troops saw the Nazi enjoy direct, effective air support while they had none. To tell men a certain bridge is gone, or ten enemy aircraft have been burned on the ground is no consolation whatever while they are being dive bombed and machine gunned. Strategic bombing has its place but it is not a great morale factor. The Army favors strategic bombing but wants its own air arm for close support.

German air operations in CRETE clearly demonstrated the terrific effectiveness of air power. Air power as delivered at CRETE is the greatest striking force known to warfare. But RAF operations in the same theatre demonstrate just as clearly that air power can be as fragile as it is strong.

The German presented his air force in mass. Overriding all resistance _regardless of cost_ it inflicted tremendous destruction. All barriers broke before it - aircraft, AA and field artillery, fleet, defending troops. On every mission _more than enough_ aircraft to accomplish the desired destruction were sent. Thirty Stukas dived on a single gun position; a dozen fighters escorted one glider flight to its objective. Operating only a few miles from their bases, hundreds of fighters and dive bombers put down continuous fire. It is estimated that 1,200 planes, unopposed by British Air Forces, participated in the attack against the Battle Fleet off KYTHERA Straits; 320 were over the fleet in one attack.

From M.A. Cairo, Egypt. Report No. 1987.   8 September 1941.

By necessity RAF substituted watch and skill for mass. With inadequate - often without - fighter protection bombers flew day missions over enemy territory. Single Hurricanes on combat missions often drew out an entire Nazi squadron; a few fighters sometimes were forced to engage a like number of squadrons. Odds against the RAF were always high. Failing to shoot the British out of the air, the German would follow to the airdrome, destroy the aircraft on the ground.

In each air engagement the RAF pilots invariably shot down more planes than they lost. But in the long run RAF air power petered out, while the German had lost but a fraction of his force.

MEDICAL:

No medical report on CRETE was made available. Numerous dispatches, however, list heavy casualties and eye witnesses claim local losses at times were heavier than any they had ever seen in the World War. Proportion of killed was low but proportion of serious and walking cases was high. There was no transportation for the evacuation of the wounded and all except walking cases were left behind. On 22 May medical supplies at RETIMO were exhausted. An attempt was made to drop some from the air but they fell in the BAY. Two days later the RETIMO garrison had lost communications by road with the other British forces. At that time they had four days' rations, 450 wounded and no medical supplies.

Due to enemy sinking of supply vessels, throughout the CRETE action medical supplies were scarce. During the CRETE operation complaints against short trousers were replete. Possibly it was because of changing temperatures, more likely from minor injuries to exposed legs due to night movements and lying in slit trenches.

LOSSES:

The 27,550 troops on CRETE 20 May were reinforced by about 1,500 troops from EGYPT. Only 14,850 of this total were evacuated. All heavy and most light weapons, including rifles, were left behind.

Naval officers estimate 75 per cent of the entire battle fleet's effectiveness was lost in the CRETE operation. Twenty-five per cent of these damages were repairable within a few months; 25 per cent more could be repaired in six or more months; the remaining 25 per cent was a total loss. In the CRETE operation every ship except the QUEEN ELIZABETH was struck, suffered varying degrees of damage. Loss of three cruisers, six destroyers and the greater portion of their crews has been announced. Four hundred soldiers were lost on the ORION.

British estimate the German lost 2,000 men sunk in caiques, 4,000 killed in battle, 8,000 wounded. German losses in planes were low considering the abandon of the attack.

In any event, the Nazi paid a small price for CRETE and the destruction and defeat he inflicted on the Royal Navy.

From M.A. Cairo, Egypt. Report No. 1987.   8 September 1941.

CONCLUSIONS:

1. That there were ample British troops to hold CRETE against the German land attack by air-borne troops; British troops were properly disposed, well led, fought desperately; it was air supply and air support which enabled the German to win.

2. That sites for airdromes must be selected with a view to their defense against air and land attacks and that, at airdromes of importance, defenses must be prepared as thoroughly as are modern harbor defenses.

3. That when overwhelming air superiority over ground troops is established, no movement is possible during daylight and troops are relegated to night operations.

4. That close support for field forces by air power is essential to insure their freedom of maneuver and success in attack.

5. That during CRETE operations the German Air Force performed roles normally assigned Services and other Arms: That of transport; of supply; of communications by signals, radio, liaison; of field, medium, and heavy artillery by bombing; of Infantry by machine gunning and tactical placement of troops; of Cavalry by reconnaissance, counter-reconnaissance, harassing, delay, follow-up, pursuit, providing the highest possible degree of mobility, delivering automatic fire power heavier than heretofore known; of Coast Artillery by denying vessels access to harbors; of Navy by its thorough defeat of the British Fleet.

6. That the numerical strength of the German Air Force was impressive; the handling of it was superb; the types of planes were suited to the task allotted.

7. That from the standpoint of ground defense the CRETE operation cannot be considered abnormal. Anywhere overwhelming air superiority is established even temporarily a similar victory over the best ground troops is possible.

8. That both Army and Naval AA failed to inflict destruction desired but as a deterrent are absolutely necessary.

9. That without taking unjustifiable losses a Navy cannot operate in waters over which the enemy controls the air.

10. That operations against the Royal Navy in CRETE waters cannot be considered abnormal in that similar losses can be inflicted on any navy which, without adequate fighter support, ventures within range of land-based dive bombers.

11. That combined operations are possible only when land-based fighter cover can be assured.

12. That sea superiority without air support is insufficient to insure success of joint overseas operation; conversely, a chain of strategically located air bases and a strong, balanced, determined air force is the best initial defense against landing operations.

From M.A. Cairo, Egypt.   Report No. 1987.   8 September 1941.

13. That based on the experience on the British during the CRETE operation it is clear that no island, or canal, on strategic area can be considered secure until all bases within effective Air Force range can be denied the enemy.

14. That the signal success of the German Air Army in CRETE has demonstrated clearly a practical solution to our problem of Hemisphere defense.

15. That the overwhelming defeat inflicted by the German Air Force on the British Fleet of KYTHERA Straits is conclusive proof of the total inability of the naval forces from one continent to dominate the territorial waters of another continental power when this second continental power has a strong air arm.

RECOMMENDATIONS:

1. That the results of the German Air Force operations against the Royal Navy off CRETE be considered by the War and Navy Departments as a solution to the defense of the UNITED STATES against a coalition of naval power superior to our fleet.

2. That the War Department consider the air logistics of the CRETE operation as a practical solution to the supply and reinforcement of our continental and insular field forces.

3. That the War Department study the German Air Army and its operation against CRETE with a view to creating an American Air Army of sufficient strength to uphold our Western Hemisphere interests and on a scale commensurate with the talent and genius and productive capacity peculiar to America.

Bonner F. Fellers
Major, G.S.
Military Attache

From M. A. Cairo, Egypt.   Report No. 1987.   8 September 1941.

INDEX TO APPENDICES

APPENDIX	TITLE	PAGES
1.	KYTHERA CHANNEL AIR-NAVAL BATTLE	1-6
2.	DEFENSE OF MALEME AIRDROME	7-10
3.	THE GERMAN ATTACK ON CRETE Headquarters, Royal Air Force, Middle East. August, 1941	11-59
4.	SERVICES COMMITTEE ON THE CAMPAIGN IN CRETE.	60-133
5.	REPORT ON AIR OPERATIONS IN CRETE 17th April - 21st May, 1941	134-187
6.	EXTRACTS FROM ROYAL AIR FORCE INTELLIGENCE SUMMARIES May 14 to May 21, 1941	188-211
7.	HEADQUARTERS, ROYAL AIR FORCE, MIDDLE EAST OPERATIONAL SUMMARY - CRETE	212-218
8.	AIRDROMES IN CRETE	219
9.	DIARY AND STATISTICS COMPILED FROM OFFICIAL SOURCES	220-234
10.	BRIEF GENERAL SUMMARY OF OPERATIONS	235-238
11.	BRITISH LOSSES IN GREECE AND CRETE	239
12.	TRANSLATION OF AN ARTICLE FROM "DER ADLER" ON THE CRETE CAMPAIGN. (Decorations awarded Germans, Crete)	240-243
13.	REPORT FROM H.M.S. "GLENGYLE" May 20, 1941	244-246
14.	REVISED TRANSLATION OF GERMAN DOCUMENTS, PROVIDED BY ARMY INTELLIGENCE DIVISION, MIDDLE EAST.	247-258

APPENDIX NO. 1

KYTHERA CHANNEL AIR-NAVAL BATTLE

KYTHERA CHANNEL AIR NAVAL BATTLE

The following notes were dictated by one who witnessed the naval engagement with the German Luftwaffe off the northwest coast of CRETE. Having previously witnessed three other engagements of a similar but vastly smaller nature, he is probably in a position to picture accurately the destruction inflicted on the fleet, the intensity of the attack, and to evaluate correctly some of the major features.

The major battle fleet in the Eastern Mediterranean moved from ALEXANDRIA harbor on the night of 18 May (Sunday) for an unknown destination in the Central Eastern Mediterranean. On the morning of the 19th the battle fleet was engaged at about 7:30 a.m. by a small squadron of German bombers escorted by long-range fighters for approximately one hour. No damage was done to the fleet during this attack but within an hour and a half it was followed by a heavier attack in which torpedoes were fired at the two battleships, VALIANT and WARSPITE. Simultaneously high level bombers operated against the fleet. Again there was no damage and only one German aircraft was shot down.

The following day, 20th May, as the fleet proceeded in a more or less northwesterly direction we were attacked seven separate times by squadrons of German high level bombers, mostly JU 88's, until approximately 6:30 in the afternoon when we approached the northwestern corner of CRETE. In a rather daring sunset attack five dive bombers of the Stuka variety dropped out from behind a small cloud formation, attacked our escorting cruisers, the ORION, AJAX and PERTH. The first Stuka peeled off its formation and dropped a large caliber bomb within a few feet of the ORION'S starboard bow. Three other Stukas in rapid succession were shot down and the fifth did not press home its attack. Only two of the five escaped.

Wednesday, 21 May, was M day for the fleet. After several destroyers and two cruisers left their formation with the battle fleet late on Monday night, 19 May, they were ordered through the KYTHERA Channel to break up by any means possible the German sea-borne invasion of CRETE. This they successfully did on 21 May, although I did not see any of the operations.

On the morning of 22 May the destroyers managed to get through the very narrow entrance of the KYTHERA Straits and rejoined the fleet at about 5:00 a.m. At 6:30 a.m. the first major attack by the German Air Force occurred. The main battle fleet was attacked by what appeared to be 24 JU 88's, some of which were carrying torpedoes. This early morning attack was beaten off by extremely heavy AA fire of the fleet but as yet we had seen no defending aircraft of the RAF. The 6:30 a.m. attack was followed almost immediately by a squadron of dive bombers operating from the southern-most islands of GREECE. Their attack was not so violent as was anticipated and although they scored several near misses there was little damage done to any of the vessels. Sporadic attacks of this kind, receiving ever increasing support from fighter aircraft, continued until about 9:30 a.m. At that time word was received by the acting flagship, WARSPITE, that two of the cruisers which had entered the KYTHERA Straits to smash the German sea-borne attempted invasion were unable to reach open sea again because one had been damaged and the other could not leave its wounded partner without serious trouble for both in view of their limited aircraft defenses. The Acting Commander-in-Chief, Admiral Rollins, then ordered the entire battle fleet, consisting of two battleships, four cruisers and approximately sixteen destroyers, to proceed to their assistance. After continuous attacks from German high level bombers operating presumably from Southern GREECE the battle fleet reached the mouth of the KYTHERA Channel at 12:15 p.m.

Aircraft continued to shatter the movements of the fleet, dropping bombs occasionally but with no damage until the battle fleet arrived near the two stranded cruisers. At approximately 1:20 p.m., with air attacks continuing constantly, the battle fleet, escorting the two cruisers, turned westward to pass through the Straits and into the open Mediterranean. At 1:30 p.m. scores of German planes appeared out of the haze, which offered them first-class opportunity to hide themselves until attack was propitious.

The first ship to be struck was the leading battleship, WARSPITE, which was attacked by three ME 109's which dived from approximately 5000 feet, not pulling out of their dive until they were about 300 feet above the WARSPITE. These planes were not observed making their attack until it was too late to open effective AA fire against them. This was true because for the first time in modern warfare high level dive bombing and torpedo bombing were combined in simultaneous efforts. Dive bombers swooped down upon ships of the fleet simultaneously as heavily loaded high level bombers were dropping loose tons and tons of bombs at all ships in the area. WARSPITE suffered one direct hit on her starboard mid-ship, presumably of about 500 to 750 pounds. The resultant explosion destroyed her engine room air ventilating system and caused considerable damage to the blower system of her engines. She was then an easy target for the hundreds of planes which by this time had appeared. Making great clouds of black smoke, WARSPITE called upon all ships of the fleet to put up what is known as an "umbrella barrage" to protect her from approximately 35 to 40 dive bombers which then made for her. None of these found its target. In the meanwhile additional planes appeared from the Greek islands which could be easily seen off our starboard bow. By 2:30 in the afternoon it was estimated that 320 planes were over the twenty or so odd ships in the Straits.

Next ship to suffer a direct hit was the destroyer GREY-HOUND, operating a short distance in the destroyer screen off VALIANT'S port bow. She received one direct hit, whether from a dive bomber or a high level bomber it was impossible to say. The bomb penetrated her aft deck, exploding in the aft magazine which, in turn, exploded with terrific force almost simultaneously with the forward magazine. The blast from this ship blew men on board my ship, the VALIANT, off their feet and several were injured as a result of blast effect and being thrown against the armor plate of the ship. Very few of the GREYHOUND crew could possibly have been alive but some, perhaps forty, were clearly visible struggling in the water. Immediately after the ship disappeared and her fuel oil began to spread over the nearby surface of the Straits, other German planes arrived firing incendiary bullets and dropping incendiary bombs on the water, setting fire to a large patch in which all hands apparently were burned to death. Another destroyer, whose name I do not know, was dispatched to GREYHOUND'S assistance but before she could arrive also was hit directly with a small caliber bomb which prevented her from engaging in further operations.

To the rear of VALIANT was a portion of the cruiser flotilla including the new AA cruiser, FIJI. FIJI, which had been engaged in steady firing of her main armament as well as smaller AA pieces, was attacked several times by dive bombers and at about 3:30 in the afternoon she ran out of ammunition. German reconnaissance planes, which kept constant vigilance over the operations of their own aircraft as well as the fleet, spotted FIJI'S inactivity and reported immediately to the bombing command. A number of German planes, estimated to be not less than sixty, then concentrated on FIJI with the result that she was struck perhaps eight or ten times in a matter of a few minutes. After reeling dizzily, with smoke pouring from her decks and funnels, FIJI capsized and sank with a struggle of less than ten minutes. The number of her survivors is still not known. German planes again swooped down on whatever men were in the nearby waters and machine gunned them for several minutes.

Either simultaneously with or within a few minutes after the cruiser GLOUCESTER was struck by a heavy caliber bomb which penetrated her aft magazine, exploding the ship in one great burst. GLOUCESTER burned for about half an hour before she finally went down. She had no survivors.

The Luftwaffe, although still overhead in numbers exceeding 150, then returned to their attack on the capital ships, WARSPITE and VALIANT. VALIANT moved alongside WARSPITE in an attempt to protect the crippled sister ship which we learned at this time had had one of her AA guns exploded by the first bomb, killing 87 men and wounding well over one hundred. VALIANT, carrying considerably more AA fire power than WARSPITE, took the brunt of the attack. By this time the sky had gotten considerably more murky but not sufficiently bad to completely destroy visibility from the air although from sea it was nearly impossible to spot a plane until it was on top of us. At 4:20 p.m. one bomb of approximately 2000 pounds fell ten feet from VALIANT'S port bow, holing the ship very badly beneath the water line and literally picking her bows out of the water and shifting her course by more than ninety degrees. As VALIANT attempted to fall back into battle line she was struck twice more directly by lighter caliber bombs which penetrated her quarter deck on the port side. The external damage to VALIANT appeared insignificant but her interior was quite badly gutted. Chief damage, however, was done by the near miss which shook loose hundreds of her plates as well as destroying a considerable portion of her under-water armor. Casualties in VALIANT amounted to about 67 fatalities to over 230 wounded, of which an additional 50 are supposed to have died since.

Throughout this engagement, which was the first major battle in history between unopposed air force and sea power, several attempts were made by the fleet to force their way through the narrows of the Strait. These were foiled largely as a result of torpedo bombers dropping hundreds of torpedoes in the narrow waters and simultaneously releasing what are believed to have been high explosive mines.

At 5:00 p.m. another of the "K" class destroyers received two direct hits from light caliber bombs across her forward deck, one of which seemed to have ricocheted through several bulkheads before exploding and finally making contact beneath the bridge. This destroyer, badly crippled and unable to keep up the rapid maneuvering of the remainder of the fleet, was deserted and left to her own devices. When last seen she was attempting gamely but feebly to beat off the attacks of an unestimated number of planes.

The skirmish, with the German air strength never seeming to diminish, continued incessantly until 8:30 p.m. when the main battle fleet, at great risk because of torpedoes and mines, finally pushed its way out of the narrows. At 6:30 the next morning we were again attacked by JU 88's which not only dive bombed but dropped torpedoes and unleashed heavy loads from altitudes beyond the range of our AA guns.

At 7:15 a.m. we received word from the destroyer, KELLY, that she was in a crippled condition just southwest of CRETE and required immediate assistance. Again the battle fleet turned back towards the KYTHERA Straits in the direction given by the KELLY. Continuous attacks were carried out for more than five hours during our return but no direct hits were scored and damage was caused only by near misses which holed AJAX, PERTH and ORION and further loosened the armor plating of the VALIANT. Upon our arrival at the destination given by KELLY'S S.O.S. the ship had disappeared. From one of her very few survivors it was learned that she went down in about 45 seconds and had only time to send the one signal previously mentioned.

Again the battle fleet turned westward and it was constantly shattered by reconnaissance planes but only one major attack was pressed home during the afternoon. At three o'clock several large formations, perhaps totalling 75 to 100 planes, closed in from all directions and bombed from high level. No dive bombers were included in this operation. Whatever damage, if any, was sustained by the fleet in this last attack resulted from bomb splinters and further loosening of the ships' structure. However, it was noticeable that despite the urgent necessity to get out of range as soon as possible the speed of the fleet was materially lessened and finally, two days later, limped into ALEXANDRIA harbor at less than 11 knots.

Naval Intelligence estimates which I have seen say that not less than 1200 of the German aircraft participated in the action against the fleet. What their losses were is apparently not known but throughout the entire action I saw only seven shot down. Practically the entire 1200, according to the same reports, operated from bases in Southern GREECE and were able in a matter of less than two hours of dropping their bombs or carrying out their torpedo attacks to return to their base, refuel, reload and return to the engagement.

Following is a report on other ships which were engaged in the battle of CRETE, all of which I have personally been on and seen since their return to ALEXANDRIA harbor. It is based on the information given me by their officers and members of the crews, plus what I personally could witness.

The cruiser ORION received two direct hits by medium caliber bombs. The first bomb penetrated her foremost (or "A") gun turret exploding in the forward magazine. The second, striking her chart house atop the bridge, penetrated six decks and exploded on the mess deck. Her total casualties - more than 750 of which 450 were fatalities. This high casualty list is due largely to the fact that she was crowded with 1100 troopers being evacuated from CRETE. The interior of the ship from well forward to as far aft as her second aft, or "X" gun turret, on two decks was burned out and practically no bulkhead was left without either being blown completely out or badly bulged by heat and blast. The blast on her forward gun turret was so great it not only destroyed the two 6-inch guns in the destroyed turret but blew the top of the turret with such force against the two guns above her on the "B" turret as to bend the muzzle of one by nearly 45 degrees. All hands in both forward gun turrets were killed instantly. Bits of bomb splinter penetrated through four or five different layers of armor plating and killed several persons, including Captain Back on the bridge.

The cruiser PERTH received one direct hit approximately amidships on her port side which penetrated three decks and exploded, killing 27 with the injured amounting to about 40. Damage to this ship was at first thought to be superficial and she was placed into service within less than a month and participated in action around the SYRIAN coast, being stationed at HAIFA. However, she proved in two engagements that she participated in off SYRIA to be unfightworthy and has since been sent home to SYDNEY for repairs. Although her decks were straightened out and repaired very rapidly, she shook badly and shipped water when she fired her own guns, thus indicating that her plates were badly sprung and that she is not expected to be a fight-worthy ship again for at least six or eight months.

The cruiser DIDO was of the same class as the FIJI, built expressly for AA action. After picking up about six hundred troops in CRETE she was attacked by a large squadron of JU 88's and Dorniers. The Dorniers participated in high level bombing while the JU 88's attacked her in what has become to be known as the "glide bombing operation". She was struck directly in almost the same position as ORION except that the bomb penetrated her "B" turret, exploding in her magazine. Casualties amounted to about 150. The number of dead has never been made known but presumably amounted to nearly half that number. I boarded the ship on her return to ALEXANDRIA and, as in the case of ORION also, acetylene torches were needed to cut away scores of sections of her interior bulkheads to get at the bodies of the dead and wounded. This was not completed for at least two days after which only high naval officials and personnel engaged in the actual work were allowed to approach the ship. Her gun muzzles also were bent and two of her forward guns were blown away by the blast of what was officially described as only a medium caliber gun.

The craft carrier FORMIDABLE was sent out two days before the major battle fleet put to sea. At that time, on highest authority, I know FORMIDABLE was carrying only six fighter aircraft. Two of these were Fulmer two-seat fighters with a top speed of 237 knots and four of them were "Swordfish", out-dated biplanes with a maximum speed of 120 miles an hour. On her second day she was attacked by 64 dive bombers and an escort of at least that number of ME 109 fighters. Her first hit was a 1500 pound bomb which penetrated her port beam a few feet below the flight deck. It smashed through six or eight bulkheads before exploding just as it was penetrating the starboard bow. The resultant hole in her starboard bow was about 29 or 30 feet in diameter but was all above the water line. More than 50 new plates were required on her starboard bow replacing those which had been destroyed before she could put to sea for a port of repair. Her casualties were small as the bomb did not explode actually within the ship but many men suffered severely from a form of shell shock or from blast.

The destroyer NUBIAN, also engaged in the evacuation of troops from CRETE, received a direct hit on her stern with approximately a 1200 pound bomb. The bomb penetrated several decks and in exploding set off NUBIAN'S depth charges, located on racks at the stern. The combined explosions blew out the entire rear section of NUBIAN and actually gave her the appearance of a fan-tail ship since her plates were so badly blown outwards and bent that she was broader at her stern than she was amidships. The rudder was lost but inexplicably her two screws remained intact and she returned to port under her own power, although she had to be towed the last 15 or 20 knots. Her total casualties were about fifty.

Battleships WARSPITE, after a month in ALEXANDRIA harbor being made ready for sea, sailed for the UNITED STATES via SUEZ CANAL. While she was somewhere between PORT SAID and SUEZ German high level bombers encountered her and scored another direct hit also amidship on her port side in relatively the same position as the hit which she had received in the battle of CRETE. Her dead were authoritatively reported at 27 and her wounded 74.

APPENDIX NO. 2

DEFENSE OF MALEME AIRDROME

Notes taken by Major Perrin, A.C.

DEFENSE OF MALEME AIRDROME

Summarization of Report:

Ground defense was laid out assuming adequate air support. The intensity and violence of the German air attack had not been visualized.

The following comments regarding the defense of Maleme airdrome were obtained from an officer present at the attack.

The 5th New Zealand Brigade had been in Greece in the Mt. Olympus area defending passes. It was withdrawn without having been engaged during the general evacuation. Although no personnel were lost most of the heavy equipment was left behind. Rifles and small stocks of ammunition were brought.

The Brigade arrived in Crete approximately 28 April. On arrival the British told the New Zealand troops to "scatter" or do anything they wanted for a day or two to relax. As a result it took two or three days to reassemble the troops.

At this time no command had been set up on Crete. Brigadier Harcourt, being the highest ranking New Zealand officer, assumed command of New Zealand troops and elected to defend the Maleme area with his Brigade.

During the three weeks prior to the Blitz, the Brigade prepared their position around the airdrome; one company dug in around the airdrome, one on the south as immediate reserves and a third south east as a tactical reserve. Deep shelters were not dug since "they never dreamed that they would not have adequate air support". In other words, the defenses were based on the assumption that air support would be furnished.

A few supplies and armament were brought to Crete during the lull. Several Bofors anti-aircraft guns, two 3-inch anti-aircraft guns, some captured Italian 75 mm. guns and a few mortars were obtained. The Bofors and 3-inch guns were placed around the airdrome, the mortars and 75's placed so as to cover the beaches.

Apparently no definite plan was evolved for a coordinated defense of the island. Commanding officers were changed each time someone with higher rank showed up until General Freyberg was named as Commander-in-Chief. His arrival was quite late and his staff was never adequate.

Small amounts of ammunition and supplies continued to arrive but never in sufficient quantities. The German air attacks on Suda Bay were more or less continuous and increasing in intensity. The delivery and unloading of supplies became more and more difficult. During the latter part of the period ships were unloaded during bombing raids and while sinking. One highlight of the occasion occurred about 17 May when, with the need for supplies and ammunition critical, the British sent a military band, complete with instruments, to bolster the morale.

All of the troops in the Brigade were not trained infantry. About 500 service corps troops and a considerable number of artillery troops were given rifles and organized in the reserves.

Immediately on the west of the Maleme airdrome is the Tavronitis River and a wooded section. Due to the lack of adequate personnel no troops were placed in this area. Some Australian and Greek troops, however, were placed on a flat plain and prison camp about four or five miles inland from Maleme. These troops were never engaged.

The RAF had some personnel, a few Gladiators and Hurricanes on the airdrome. All of these were destroyed, the majority while on the ground, prior to 19 May. German attacks on Maleme, however, were not particularly intense until 20 May. Daily reconnaissance had been made and, as it turned out, extremely accurate information regarding the New Zealand troop and gun positions had been gotten.

At about 6:30 on the morning of 20 May the Blitz began. For about one and a half hours the attack by JU 87's and 88's, and ME 109's and 110's was continuous. The airplanes, flying low, attacked gun positions, ground troop positions and buildings. The crew of the anti-aircraft guns went to their slit trenches at the beginning of the attack and never returned. Not over two or three anti-aircraft shots were fired. Upon evacuating the area of Maleme airdrome, nothing was destroyed and later the Germans used the Bofors against the British.

Lieutenant Mason described the attack as an "Intense artillery bombardment carried on by aircraft". After this one and a half hours preparation the intensity of the Blitz lessened and parachute troops were dropped. German fighters covered their descent by continuing the strafing of the ground troops. The parachute troops were landed on the airdrome and in the river bed and woods to the west.

Six hundred to eight hundred parachutists were dropped the first day. The airdrome was captured together with some RAF secret codes. The New Zealanders counter attacked and succeeded in killing most of the Germans on the airdrome. Those in the river bed and woods were not destroyed and during the night consolidated their position.

Immediately upon landing the Germans set up a radio and were able to contact their aircraft to ask for and direct operations against New Zealand strong points and gun installations.

On the 21st the Germans started pouring troops into the Maleme area. More parachutists were dropped. Gliders were towed in, the majority landing along the river, and JU 52's were landed on the airdrome and beach. Lieutenant Mason did not know the number of gliders used but stated that six hundred air transport loads of troops were landed. Landings were accomplished under fire of the New Zealand 75's and mortars.

Almost each German section leader had a small map of the Maleme area showing the New Zealand positions, areas in which parachute troops were to land and the direction of effort each one of the groups of troops were to make.

As a result of the German reinforcements the New Zealanders withdrew from their positions immediately adjacent to the airdrome to their reserve defenses.

On the 22nd the number of transport troops decreased, gliders were not used and only a few parachute troops were landed. These latter, however, were dropped in strategic points.

Brigadier Harcourt decided to withdraw from the Maleme area entirely. Ammunition and supplies were running low and the New Zealanders were outnumbered. They withdrew during the night toward Canea. From the night of the 22nd until the final evacuation from Sphakia the story was the same, withdrawal by night, digging in and fighting rear guard action by day. On one occasion they found it necessary to withdraw by day. The Germans had gone around their flank during the night and set up machine guns covering the line of retreat. Two companies of Mauries were sent out to silence the machine guns (which they did, losing only two men) while the remainder withdrew. On several occasions the Germans partially flanked the New Zealanders and groups were sent out to silence them. The majority of these groups never returned to the main body and it is doubtful if they ever managed to leave the island.

       The Brigade reached Sphakia the night of 30 May with less than half of the troops they had at Maleme, no food and no ammunition. Until they reached Sphakia they did not know whether they would be evacuated or not.

       During the entire battle and withdrawal there had been no coordinated action with other units. Communications were practically nonexistent.

APPENDIX NO. 3

THE GERMAN ATTACK ON CRETE

Headquarters, Royal Air Force, Middle East

August, 1941

THE GERMAN ATTACK ON CRETE

FORENOTE

The object of this report is to assemble the information obtained with regard to German plans and methods in the attack on CRETE, with particular reference to parachutists and glider troops.

The material used in the report consists principally of captured documents, prisoner of war statements, reports by personnel from Greece and official reports.

A large number of documents were captured in CRETE. Unfortunately, the major part were subsequently lost and only a very small proportion were ultimately available for trained intelligence examination. Fortunately, these included a number of most useful documents relating to the attack on CRETE including Regimental orders, details of gliders and parachutes and signals organization. The more important captured documents are reproduced as appendices to this report.

The information obtained from captured documents has been completed by intelligence obtained from prisoners of war, reports from British Personnel in CRETE and official reports. As far as possible, however, original (German) sources have been used.

The report is divided into two parts. Part I (Operational) deals with the German preparations and plan of attack and in summarised form, with the actual attack. Part 2 (Tactical and Technical) puts together the information obtained regarding the employment of glider troops, parachutists and air-borne troops in CRETE, and the Signals organization employed.

Appendices includes captured documents, maps and photos, together with reference maps.

H.Q., R.A.F., M.E., 'I'
August 1941

SECTION I

The decision to attack CRETE by air and the choice of units to be employed had already been made by the middle of April, i.e., during the early part of the campaign in GREECE. Captured diaries and prisoner of war reports show that preparations were already under way in the third week of April.

Many of the air landing troops ultimately employed in the capture of CRETE were already in the BALKANS in March, and took part in the operations in YUGO-SLAVIA and GREECE during April, but the parachute and glider troops of Fliegerdivision VII were apparently brought down specially for the CRETE operation.

The move was made during the last week of April and the first fortnight of May. Some units travelled by rail direct from GERMANY to SALONIKA; others travelled part of the distance by rail and completed the journey by road. The movement of these units was given special priority everywhere, indicating a high degree of urgency. In spite of this, traffic on roads and railways was so congested that units took 10-14 days to make the journey to Northern GREECE. Some of the glider units flew down all the way from GERMANY to SALONIKA in easy stages of 200 kms. a day.

The gliders were concentrated originally in the SALONIKA area. No. 1 Coy. of Storm Regt. I, 15 gliders, together with pilots, fitters and riggers arrived at SALONIKA by rail on May 10th. The gliders were unloaded on the following day and by May 15th were all fitted and rigged. On May 14th a further 60 gliders arrived by air. This completed the glider force and on May 16th the entire regiment flew down from SALONIKA to TANAGRA, the distance of approximately 150 miles being covered in 1 hour, 25 minutes.

The parachute units are believed to have been concentrated in the first instance in BULGARIA in the SORIA and PLOVDIV areas. They were moved down to Souther GREECE by rail and road in the second week of May.

continued ...

-12-

SECTION I

The JU.52 transport aircraft necessary on the operation appear to have moved down to the BALKANS in the second half of April, and to have been held in readiness in the SOFIA, PLOVDIV and BUCHAREST areas until required. They only moved down to the operational bases in the ATHENS and SALONIKA areas a few days before the actual operation.

During May, supplies of petrol, bombs and other stores were forwarded urgently to the ATHENS area by road, rail and sea. By the middle of May, troops, gliders and stores had been assembled in GREECE and final preparations were being made.

Security

Stringent security measures were enforced during the journey. Parachutists were ordered to remove badges; exchange pay books for identity cards; exchange driving licences for provisional driving permits; discard parachutist's uniform during the journey; they were forbidden to carry private papers; to purchase or post cards or letters; battalion crests and other distinctive markings were to be removed from M.T. etc.; finally (supreme indignity) they were forbidden to sing parachutist's songs. A doctor attached to the 2nd Battalion Storm Regt. (Glider troops) notes in his diary that on April 18th he was in the middle of preparations, adding that details of inoculations were to be sent by teleprinter for greater secrecy.

The general level of security must have been very good, as in spite of the fact that in the last few days before the operation some hundreds of persons at least must have known of the intended operation, and despite the concentration of troops, aircraft and gliders for the operation, the secret appears to have been well kept.

Preparation of Bases

By the capture of GREECE the Germans obtained aerodromes suitable for long range bombers and transport at SALONIKA and LARISSA in Northern GREECE, THEBES, MENIDI, ELEUSIS, TANAGRA, HASSANI and CORINTH in the ATHENS area, but for short range fighters and dive bombers it was necessary to have bases nearer to CRETE. Immediately after the capture of GREECE, even before our forces had been fully mopped up, reconnaissance was started for suitable sites in the South

SECTION I

of the PELEPPONNESE and on the Islands of the Southern AGEAN. A site was found at MULOIA in Southern GREECE and was in use within a week. Ground staff for work on this aerodrome were flown down in four JU 52's. Another site was found on MELOS Island which was occupied on April 10th and work was begun the same day, British prisoners and local labour being employed. The existing landing ground on SCARPANTO Island was enlarged and improved. By the middle of April the Germans had at least three aerodromes within little more than 100 miles of CRETE.

DISPOSITION OF AIRCRAFT

The final disposition of aircraft in preparation for the attack was as follows:-

<u>Germans</u> Dive Bombers   MOLAOI, ARGOS, CORINTH,
                                        SCARPANTO, MILOS

         Single-engine fighters   MOLAOI, MILOS, CORINTH,
                                        ARGOS

         Long range fighters   ARGOS, CORINTH and ATHENS area

         Long range bombers   ATHENS (ELEUSIS and MENIDI),
         and recce.   SALONIKA (SEDES and MIKRA),
                                        BULGARIA (KROMOVO and PLOVEIV),
                                        RHODES

         Transport aircraft   ATHENS (ELEUSIS, MENIDI),
                                        MEGARA, CORINTH, PERIVALI,
                                        TANAGRA, TOPOLIA, SALONIKA
                                        (SEDES and MIKRA).

Preliminary Recces and Air Attacks over CRETE

In the meantime the objective was being targetted with Teutonic thoroughness. In the first half of May German aircraft reconnoitred the island practically daily. Photographs captured later show that very thorough photographic reconnaissance was carried out of our positions and defences during this period. The target maps of HERAKLION (See Appendix " " " ") appears to have been taken about 2 weeks before the invasion. Captured photographs and maps bore markings indicating our gun positions and defences, and in some cases arrows indicate the line of approach and the point of attack (see Appendix " ").

In the first half of May attacks were maintained against our

-14-

SECTION I

shipping and sea communications around the Island. The landing of supplies became almost impossible. Of 27,700 tons of supplies sent to the Island, 21,600 tons were turned back, 3,400 tons were sunk and only 2,700 tons were unloaded. A number of ships were sunk in SUDA BAY harbour. Even before the attack the supply problem was acute. In the middle of May it was apparently decided to neutralise our fighter forces on the island, which had been battling bravely against great odds. From May 13th, systematic attacks were carried out against our aerodromes and fighter aircraft in CRETE. Reinforcements were not at the time available in EGYPT, and owing to the distance, fighter support from our bases in North AFRICA was impracticable. On May 15th after heavy losses had been sustained it was decided to withdraw the remaining aircraft to EGYPT. This was effected on May 19th (the day before the invasion), by which date only seven fighters remained serviceable.

During the last few days before the attack, the Germans intensified their attacks on our A.A. positions and batteries, with the double object of probing our defences and reducing the morale of our troops. These attacks were usually carried out at intervals throughout the day, with a special "hate" at dawn and dusk. High level bombing, dive bombing and ground strafing tactics were employed in turn, the attacks being directed in particular against gun crews. The damage and casualties caused by these preliminary attacks were not heavy, but the continued strain on the gun crews had its effect upon their morale. As our fighter aircraft were eliminated the enemy became bolder. During the last few days before the invasion, aircraft came down as low as 500 feet over the aerodromes.

By the middle of May, all major preparations had been made and final details of the attack were being worked out.

Final Preparations

On 16th May, glider units left SALONIKA for TANAGRA (ATHENS area), the gliders flying with their pilots and riggers.

On 17th May the pilots were told their objective (CRETE) and their exact position in the attacking force. In the evening General

SECTION I

STUDENT arrived and spoke with each glider pilot.

On 18th May, a conference of platoon leaders, senior N.C.O's of parachute units, JU.52 and glider pilots was held. The objectives were discussed in detail and each glider pilot was told his line of approach and the exact point at which he must land. The following day (19th May) was spent in loading preparations and in the priming of hand grenades and explosives. In the afternoon the attack was discussed once more. Detailed target maps and photographs were studied and final details decided.

Simultaneously, parachutists and air landing units were receiving their final instructions and making final preparations. All units participating were issued with orders indicating their exact part in the operation. (Several of these orders, including Regimental Battalion and Company Orders of the 1st Parachute Regt. were later captured in CRETE. They are a model of thoroughness and detailed preparation). (See Appendix " ").

Other preparations included the issue of a phrase sheet of useful sentences in German and English (with phonetic spelling), the first sentence being "If yu lei you will bi schott (If you lie you will be shot) ..."Wenn Sie lugen werden Sie erschessen".

As a final preparation before the attack, Me.109's and dive bombers made repeated attacks on MALEME aerodrome on May 19th (zero day minus one). Dive bombers attacked shipping in the harbours and recce aircraft covered the whole of the Island, paying particular attention to the possibility of dispersed troops or aircraft in the olive groves in the North-West part of the Island.

Parachutist's equipment and containers for the first wave of parachutists were loaded into the transport aircraft on the 19th, ready for the following day. The embarkation of parachutists started at 0445 on the 20th.

SECTION II

PLAN OF ATTACK

"Fliegerkorps XI will capture the Island of CRETE and hold it until relieved by German army troops of the 5th Mountain Division." (Extract from captured German operational order).

For the capture of the Island O.C., Fliegerkorps XI (General Student) was allocated glider troops and parachutists from Fliegerdivision VII and air landing troops (including a proportion of parachutists) from 5th Mountain Division and 22nd Division.

Air support was to be provided by Fliegerkorps VIII.

The plan on broad lines was to land glider troops and parachutists at selected points along the north coast of the Island, capture the aerodromes and ports at MALEME, CANEA, RETIMO and HERAKLION and prepare the way for the arrival of air landing and sea-borne troops who were to complete the capture of the Island and provide a garrison.

The forces originally allocated for the operation are estimated to have been as follows:-

Glider-borne troops	750
Parachutists	10,000
Air-landing troops	12,000
Sea-borne troops	7,500
	30,250

In view of the fact that the Germans believed that we had only 5,000 British troops on the Island, and that the Islanders were friendly, these forces must have appeared ample.

The attacking forces for the initial attack were divided into three groups, named respectively the Central, Western and Eastern Groups, the most important being the Central Group which was to attack the CANEA area where the bulk of our forces were believed to be concentrated.

SECTION II

Group	O. C.	Objective
Central Group	Maj. Gen. Suessman	CANEA-RETIMO area
Western Group	Maj. Gen. Meindl	MALEME
Eastern Group	Gen. Ringel	HERAKLION

Maj. Gen. SUESSMAN was O.C. 7th Fliegerdivision. (He was killed in a glider crash in the attack).

Maj. Gen. MEINDL is reported to have been in charge of all gliders in GREECE and CRETE.

At a later stage in the operation, on the arrival of 5th Mountain Division, it was provided that O.C., 100 Mountain Rifle Regt. should take over at MALEME and O.C., 85 Mountain Rifle Regt. at HERAKLION. This is in accordance with the general principle that 5th Mountain Division would take over from XI Fliegerkorps.

The operation was given the code name "MERKUR" (Mercury!) On the day of the attack zero hour was to be indicated by the signal "MERKUR" which would be given when the first glider was over its objective.

The plan of attack as revealed by captured documents was as follows :-

(a) <u>Preliminary air attack</u> for one hour before zero on our positions south and west of CANEA, on the AKROTIRI Peninsula and at MALEME.

(b) Landing of gliders at zero hour as follows :-

<u>Central Group</u>. One Company (15 gliders, 150 troops) on AKROTIRI Peninsula. Objective: to destroy all A.A. batteries, occupy the Royal Villa and high ground in the south-west of the AKROTIRI Peninsula. One Company (1r gliders, 150 troops) South and West of CANEA. Objective:- to destroy all AA batteries in the area South of CANEA

SECTION II

and put the wireless station out of action.

Western Group. Three companies (45 gliders, 450 troops) in river valley west of MALEME aerodrome. Objective: to occupy the area west of the aerodrome and to provide covering fire for the arrival of parachute troops.

(c) Landing of Parachutists. This was to take place in two waves:-

(i) The first wave in the morning, starting at zero hour - 15 minutes, as follows:-

Central Group. Three battalions Parachute Regt. 3 and Regimental H.Q., together Parachute Engineers Unit, A.A. M.G. Unit, Parachute Medical and Signals Units to be dropped west and south of CANEA. Time of landing 1 hour. Number of troops (estimated) 2,500. Objective: to occupy the area west and south of CANEA bounded by AG. MARINOS to the west, ALIKIANOU to the southwest and TSIKALARIA to the southeast. All communications to be cut.

Western Group. One battalion Parachute Regt. 2 to land at RETIMO. Objective: to capture the aerodrome and town and cut communications.

Eastern Group. Three battalions Parachute Regt. 1 to land at HERAKLION. Objective: to seize the town and aerodrome and cut communications.

It is estimated that 750 glider troops and 4,500 parachutists were to be dropped in the morning, and a further 3,000 parachutists in the afternoon on the first day of the attack.

As soon as possible after capturing their local objectives, these forces were to throw out patrols and endeavour to join forces until a continuous link was established along the north coast from HERAKLION to MALEME.

SECTION II

It was anticipated that the glider and parachutust attack would result in the capture of aerodromes, beaches and ports which would enable further troops to be ferried over by air and sea. These comprised elements of Fliegerdivision VII (2,500 troops), 5th Mountain Division (10,000 troops) and 22nd Division (7,500 troops) a total of 20,000 troops.

(d) Air Landing troops were to follow as soon as aerodromes had been captured. In the MALEME area it was intended to land air landing troops shortly after the first wave of the attack, on the first morning and to follow up with the landing of three battalions of Mountain Rifle Regiment 100 in the afternoon.

(e) Sea-borne troops. Two sea-borne expeditions were prepared, a "light" convoy and a "heavy" convoy. These were to bring over the heavier units of Fliegerdivision VII, (Parachute Artillery Battery, Parachute Anti-tank Unit, Parachute A.A. Artillery Unit, Parachute Motor-Cycle Battalion, Parachute M.G. Battalion, Parachute Signals, Medical and Supply Units), elements of 5th Mountain Division and (probably) 22nd Division. It was anticipated that sea-borne troops and equipment would be landed within 48 hours of the initial attack. 100 Mountain Rifle Regt. was to land at MALEME and 85 Mountain Rifle Regt. at HERAKLION.

The information available regarding the units to be carried over by sea is not complete. On the basis of such information as is available, it may be estimated that some 7,500 troops were intended to be carried in the first two convoys.

Assuming that no further convoys were intended, this would leave a further 12,500 troops to be ferried over by air. It may, however, have been the intention of the German High Command to use

SECTION II

more sea transport and correspondingly less air transport. In actual fact when the time came, the two sea convoys were intercepted and broken up with heavy loss. For several days during the most critical part of the campaign, the Germans had to rely entirely upon air transport.

Air support was to be provided by Fliegerkorps VIII and a force of 280 bombers, 150 dive bombers, 90 twin-engined fighters, 90 single-engined fighters and 40 Recces was concentrated in GREECE, BULGARIA and the AEGEAN Islands. The tasks allotted to Fliegerkorps VIII included tactical reconnaissances, fighter protection to troop carrying aircraft, attacks on our positions before and during glider and parachute descents, co-operation with ground forces, protection of sea-borne convoys and attacks on our naval and supply shipping.

SECTION III

FORCES ENGAGED

1. Forces originally provided:

The forces originally provided for the attack are estimated to have been as follows:-

Troops   (a)   Units.   Elements of:-

      XI Fliegerkorps

      VII Fliegerdivision

      5th Mountain Division

      22nd Division

  (b)   Numbers

Glider troops	750
Parachutists	7500
Air-landing troops	12500
Sea-borne troops	7500
	30750

Transport Aircraft

Type	Units	Number
Gliders D.F.S. 230	Storm Regt. I.	75
Glider towing JU.52's	Luftlandungs Geschwader I.	75
Troop Transport Aircraft	K.G. Z b V 2) 40) 60) 101) 102) 105) 106) 172)	500

Air Support.   Fliegerkorps VIII

Bombers	DO. 17, JU. 88, He.111	280
Dive Bombers	JU. 87	150
Twin-engined fighters	ME. 110	90
Single-engined fighters	ME. 109	90
Recce	DO. 17, DO. 215, He. 111 JU. 88, ME. 110	40
		650

SECTION III

Modification during the Operation

During the course of the operation the following modifications were made to the attacking and supporting forces as originally planned:-

1. Some 2500 troops (and much material) were lost at sea and never reached CRETE.

2. Elements of an additional division, 6th Mountain Division, believed to include MT; Rifle Regts. 141 and 143 were added as reinforcements in view of the unexpected strength of our opposition.

3. As the result of the interception of the first two sea convoys, the Germans had to rely entirely upon air transport to send reinforcements and supplies to CRETE. Sea transport was not re-established until May 28th, by which time our evacuation had already started.

4. Reinforcements of dive bombers were brought down from Germany and bombers from SICILY and LIBYA were diverted from operations in North Africa to CRETE. It is estimated that during the course of the operation 120 bombers and dive bombers were added to the air forces attacking CRETE. The total number of supporting aircraft engaged was therefore (excluding losses) 770.

Forces employed

It is estimated that from the start of the operation (May 20th) to the commencement of our evacuation (May 28th) the following forces were actually landed in CRETE. Deduction has been made of 2,500 estimated lost at sea.

- 23 -

SECTION III

Troops:

Glider troops	750
Parachutists	10,000
Air-landing troops	23,000
Sea-borne troops	250
Total	34,000

On May 28th and following days, sea-borne forces landed together with tanks, artillery and other heavy equipment. It is estimated that the number of tanks landed by sea probably did not exceed 5,000. The campaign was already in its closing stages and the Germans were already beginning to move troops northwards towards the Russian frontier.

Air Forces:

Gliders	75
Glider tugs	75
Transport aircraft	500
Bombers, fighters and recce.	770

SECTION IV

THE ATTACK

The attack began on May 20th. Gliders and parachutists took off from Greek aerodromes at first dawn. They were preceded by bombers, dive bombers and fighters which subjected our positions at MALEME and CANEA to an attack of terrific intensity for an hour before the air-borne forces arrived. The bombardment began at 0700 hours. It was directed particularly against gun crews and positions, with special attention to A.A. batteries, and was apparently designed to put the gun crews out of action rather than the guns themselves. The attacks were of such intensity that all troops in the area were driven to ground.

An hour later, at 0800 hrs., the gliders arrived escorted by fighters and dive bombers. Three companies landed at MALEME; a fourth South of CANEA and a fifth on the AKROTIRI Peninsula. In the meantime enemy bombing and machine gun attacks had scarcely slackened, and the area around each landing place was covered by waves of continuous attacks. It had been expected that the barrage would lift before parachutes or glider troops began to descend, and both at MALEME and CANEA where our troops had been driven to cover by the sustained intensity of the air attack, the landing of gliders was effected unperceived and unopposed.

The majority of the gliders at MALEME came down in the dried up river bed to the West of the aerodrome. It is estimated that 45 gliders were used in this area, each glider carrying 10 troops. The sunken river bed was protected from the direct line of fire from the aerodrome, and boulders and rocks there gave cover to the descending forces. The gliders crash-landed among the rocks and the troops took positions on the high ground to the West of the valley overlooking the aerodrome. Before our defenders in that area were aware of their presence, and could take action against them, they were in a strong position with formidable fire power. They were thus able to give fire cover to the arrival of the parachute troops.

SECTION IV

In the AKROTIRI Peninsula 11 gliders arrived over the objective at about 0800 hrs. (One report states that gliders arrived in the dark at 0300 hours, but there is no evidence of this in the plan of attack or from other sources). Several crashed on landing, killing and wounding a number of the personnel; three or four were shot down by our troops, one of the later exploding in the air as a result of a direct hit on the ammunition store in the forward compartment of the glider. The greater part of the glider-borne troops were killed or captured soon after landing. A few were able to install themselves in strong defensive positions (one group occupied a disused battery position) and to hold out. In view of their heavy fire power the nuisance value of these groups was out of all proportion to their numbers.

The 2nd Company Storm Regt. was ordered to destroy ALL enemy A.A. batteries in the area south of CANEA. From 0700 hours to 0800 hours on May 20th, this area was dive bombed and machine-gunned for an hour, after which gliders landed all round and on our gun positions. The gun crews had been driven to shelter by the air attack and the landing of the gliders were effected unperceived. Complete surprise was effected and the gun detachments were killed. The guns were then put out of action by a thermite preparation applied to the breach mechanism. The glider troops having thus prepared the way for the arrival of parachutists, were able to give the latter covering fire support on their arrival a few minutes later.

The landing of parachutists on the first day of the attack took place in two main waves. The first wave in the morning was directed against CANEA and MALEME where parachutists followed glider troops. The second was in the afternoon, aimed at the capture of RETIMO and HERAKLION.

SECTION IV

In the CANEA area, the first wawe of parachutists began to arrive according to plan at 0815 hours, fifteen minutes after the gliders. During the next two hours, 3 battalions of parachute troops together with H.Q. signals, engineers and medical units were dropped west and south of the town. Some temporary success was achieved and during the morning the enemy succeeded in capturing the General Hospital and occupying one of the beaches. Vigorous counter measures on our part, however, re-establishing the situation in our favour. The hospital was re-taken and before the end of the day most of the troops had been cleaned up, with the exception of a force which succeeded in establishing itself in a valley some two miles southwest of CANEA, and of scattered groups holding strong local positions. During the morning, GENERAL SUESSMAN, O.C. Fliegerkorps VII who was O.C. in the wadi Central Sector was killed, together with a number of members of his staff, when the glider in which they were traveling crashed. In the MALEME area, parachutists were dropped to west of the aerodrome, also on and near the aerodrome itself. Those who dropped on or near the aerodrome were rapidly liquidated but the others who landed to the west of the aerodrome were protected by the covering fire of the glider troops already landed and were able to consolidate their position. By mid-day, enemy troops were established on the western fringe of the aerodrome.

During the morning, some 24 Ju.52's crash-landed on the beaches east and west of MALEME, and landed two companies of troops. In the afternoon, despite the fact that our forces were still in position round the eastern end of the aerodrome, troop-carrying aircraft began to land near the western edge of the landing ground under cover of protective fire from troops established in that area. The operation must have been extremely hazardous: the landing area was under both small arms and artillery fire from our troops only a few hundred yards away, but action on our part was nullified by enemy air forces which maintained continuous attacks on our forces and pinned them to the ground. During the afternoon three battalions of Mountain Rifle Regiments 100 were landed.

SECTION IV

Towards evening, the Germans, reinforced by the new arrivals began to intensify their pressure on our position east of the aerodrome. At 2000 hours under the double pressure of air and ground attack, we were obliged to retire, leaving the aerodrome in German hands.

In the meantime, during the afternoon, the second wave of parachutists had been landed, this time at RETIMO and HERAKLION.

At RETIMO, two battalions of parachute troops were dropped, for the most part near the eastern boundary of the aerodrome. They were immediately attacked and heavy casualties were inflicted. By the evening the situation here was well in hand.

At HERAKLION, following the usual preliminary "blitz" No. 1 Parachute Regt. began to arrive at 1800 hrs. Parachutists were dropped in two groups, one round the aerodrome and the other west of the town. For some time after landing they were very vulnerable and on the aerodrome a large number were killed by tanks, small arms and bayonet within a few minutes of landing. The parachutists who dropped near HERAKLION attempted to capture the town, but were driven back by the Greeks. By the evening, the position in this area too, was well in hand.

At the end of the first day, the position was briefly as follows: At MALEME, some 750 Glider troops, 7,500 parachutists and 2,000 air landing troops had been landed, some success had been achieved and the aerodrome was in German hands, though it was still under artillery and rifle fire from our troops. In the CANEA, RETIMO and HERAKLION areas on the other hand, the parachute landings had failed to achieve their object and heavy casualties had been sustained by the attacking force.

On the second day, the remaining parachute troops were dropped, chiefly in the CANEA area, where the situation remained confused. At RETIMO, successful attacks by Australian and Greek troops drove the enemy out of the defended area round the aerodrome.

SECTION IV

At HERAKLION, the greater part of the remaining enemy forces were mopped up.

The main interest of the campaign, however, was already centring round MALEME. During the morning troop landing aircraft began to arrive at the aerodrome. In spite of the fact that the aerodrome was under artillery and, at extreme range, small arms fire, they continued to arrive throughout the day with almost clock-like regularity. In the meantime enemy air forces maintained unceasing attacks on our troops and gun positions. It was a grim battle. But one by one our gun positions were sought out and bombed into silence, while more and more troop carriers came and disgorged their troops and supplies.

Sea-borne Forces

On May 22/23rd, two German sea-borne convoys were due to arrive in CRETE bringing reinforcements, artillery, motor-cycles, cars and probably tanks. The first was sunk by our naval forces in the night May 21/22, the 2nd was scattered the following day. None of the ships reached CRETE. Much equipment and 2,500 picked troops are believed to have been lost. With the exception of one caique and a few small boat loads of survivors from the wrecked convoy, no enemy sea-borne troops reached CRETE until the 28th May, by which time the operation was virtually over.

At this point the enemy must have been obliged rapidly to re-cast his plans. He did so, as always, by reinforcing success. The local success at MALEME was exploited until MALEME rapidly became the key point of the campaign. Transport by sea had failed - so air transport must be used instead. Throughout the following day, May 22nd, troop carriers continued to land in an unending stream. Our guns were still shelling the aerodrome but our batteries had been seriously weakened, and the enemy air attacks against the remaining positions never slackened.

SECTION IV

As the German forces were strengthened, they exerted constantly increasing pressure eastwards against our forces who were holding a ridge two miles to the east of the aerodrome and overlooking it. Towards evening, we were forced to retire from the ridge. The enemy had gained uninterrupted use of the aerodrome.

The action now developed rapidly to an almost inevitable conclusion. Day after day the Germans poured in by air more troops, supplies, guns, motorcycles, ammunition. The forces originally chosen for the operation were reinforced by elements of a further division - 6th Mountain Division. Transport aircraft now landed 3 at a time, bringing units complete with equipment. In the air enemy aircraft maintained constant activity and patrol. Every movement was harassed, every exposure was dangerous. On our side, our air force, limited in numbers and obliged to operate from bases in North Africa was unable to provide the air support which alone could have turned the scales. For a variety of reasons, the strength of our air forces in North Africa was at a particularly low ebb just at that time. But even if much larger air forces had been available, they could not have overcome the geographical fact that German Fighters and Dive Bombers were operating from aerodromes almost within sight of CRETE, while our nearest bases were in North Africa 300 miles away. During the whole of the CRETE campaign, the Germans had complete and practically undisputed air superiority. Without this air superiority, the attack would have failed in its early stages. With it the Germans had been able to obtain a foothold on the island. They were now in a position to pour in reinforcements and supplies as required, while denying to us the possibility of receiving either. Once such a position was established, the ultimate result could no longer be in doubt.

During the following days enemy pressure eastwards from MALEME never relaxed. Day by day further reinforcements arrived by air to strengthen the enemy's forces. On May 26th the Germans broke through to CANEA. Our position rapidly deteriorated and

SECTION IV

preparations began to be made for evacuation ~~with~~ great difficulty SUDA BAY was covered for a night to enable a small force of reinforcements to be landed, but from the 28th, it was realized that the situation was beyond remedy and the evacuation began. The enemy air force now transferred its attention to back areas and bombed the roads to the South, and SPHAKIA and other ports on the South coast. Their scale of air attack in this final phase was not, however, as heavy as might have been expected. It is probable that some of the units were already being transferred northwards to the Russian frontier. Evacuation from SPHAKIA took place on the 3 nights May 30th, 31st and June 1st, without serious interference from the enemy.

While the main German effort was concentrated on the MALEME sector, operations in the other sectors developed more slowly. At HERAKLION the survivors of the original parachutist force established themselves in two groups outside the defended area, one to the east of the aerodrome, the other to the west of the town. During the next few days these two groups were supplied by air, and some reinforcements were dropped. On May 22nd, in the evening parachutists were dropped to the east of the aerodrome and a ridge 2 miles east of the aerodrome was occupied. From this ridge the Germans were able to cover the aerodrome with fire from heavy machine guns and mortars which had been landed by parachute earlier in the day. On May 23 further parachutists were dropped and on the same day the town of HERAKLION was bombed. During the following days the enemy gradually built up his forces. Troop-carrying aircraft found a landing place on the beach near MALEA, 15 miles east of HERAKLION. Patrols from the 2 forces east and west of HERAKLION pushed forward through a wide circle south of our positions, established contact and cut off our communications inland. The position was now judged ready for a final assault. On May 28th in the evening, a large number of parachutists were landed east of the aerodrome. The intended attack was forestalled, however, by the evacuation by sea of our garrison the same night.

SECTION IV

At RETIMO, after the failure of the initial attack, the Germans contented themselves by taking up position east of the aerodrome and west of the town, thus cutting communications with HERAKLION and CANEA. All land lines were cut and as the W/T was out of order, the garrison was completely isolated. On May 22nd a company of parachute troops was dropped and established itself to the west of the aerodrome. During the next few days German operations in this area were on a very limited scale.

On May 28th, a German convoy arrived by sea at CANEA, bringing reinforcements and tanks. The arrival of this sea-borne force had little effect on the main operations, as our forces were already in retreat, but on May 29th German forces supported by tanks attacked RETIMO. At first the garrison thought that these were our own tanks that had broken through, and it was not until they were among them that their mistake was discovered. The entire garrison was either killed or captured.

Italian participation

The Italian share in the campaign was limited to recce flights east of HERAKLION and attacks on our shipping east and south of the island. On May 28th, when the campaign was all but over, one or two regiments of Italian troops landed at SITEIA on the northeast coast. In the following days they moved across the centre of the Island westwards and joined up with the German forces in the rear of our troops on the last day of our evacuation from SPHAKIA.

PART 2   SECTION V.

TACTICAL AND TECHNICAL   GLIDERS

Organization of Glider Units.

The Glider units employed in CRETE belonged to No. 1 Storm Regt. This regiment consists of 2 battalions of 4 companies, each company having 145 to 150 men, and being divided into 5 sections or platoons of 30 men each. Each section is carried by 3 gliders (D.F.S. 230 ten-seater glider is standard equipment) and each company by 15 gliders.

In the CRETE operation all 4 companies of No. 1 Battalion were employed. The Storm Regt. was under the command of Fliegerdivision VII which, in turn, was under the operational command of Fliegerkorps XI.

References to a Glider geschwader have been received from prisoners of war and other sources. A German Glider pilot killed in CRETE is known to have belonged since September, 1940 to Staffel 5 of Gruppe 2 of Luftlandungs geschwader 1. It may therefore be tentatively accepted that at least 2 Gruppen of a Glider Geschwader (Luftlandungs - geschwader) exist.

Information from prisoners of war and captured documents establishes the fact that in the Luftlandungs geschwader there are 15 Gliders to a Staffel. The glider Staffel is thus equivalent to the glider company in the Storm Regt.

No direct evidence is available of the connection between the Storm Regt. and the Luftlandungs geschwader 1, but it seems probable that Glider Staffeln allocated to the Storm Regt. are drawn from L. 1. G. 1. i.e., that the Luftlandungs geschwader is the training unit and the Storm Regiment the operational unit.

Qualified glider pilots are given the title L.S. Fuhrer (Lastensegelflugzoug fuhrer), i.e., load carrying glider pilot. (L.S. or Load carrying glider is apparently the name given to weight carrying gliders capable of transporting men and/or materials, to distinguish

SECTION V

them from single-seater gliders with no transport capacity)

Glider troops count with parachutists as "Fliegertruppen," but glider troops are never used as parachutists and parachutists are never carried in gliders.

Training

The main training center is at HILDESHEIM, where a Deutsche Ferschungsanstalt fur Segelflugzeuge (German Glider Experimental and Research Establishment) has been in operation since before November 1939. There is evidence that in the autumn of 1940 a reorganization of Glider Units in the Storm Regt. took place, and volunteers from A.A. and Infantry units were gathered at HILIESHEIM. Intensive training of both glider pilots and glider-borne troops of the Storm Regt. has been in progress since that date. Training schools for pilots exist at BRUNS-WICK-WAGGUN, MUNSTER-WALDE, ROHN and (unconfirmed) at HALIERSTADT.

Of three glider pilots captured or killed in CRETE, two held long term commissions in the German Air Force and the third (killed) had a civil flying licence, and had transferred from a Flak Unit to Gliders in July, 1940. The first two had been flying gliders since the age of fifteen. All three had non-operational experience of power-driven aircraft, and one had even completed a course on heavy power-driven aircraft after he had joined his glider unit. Glider pilots, however, are not ranked as G.A.F. pilots. In fact some of them appear to be men who have been unable to complete successfully the full training course of G.A.F. pilots.

Some of the glider pilots employed in the CRETE operation claim to have completed 8,000 kms. in gliders.

Glider-borne troops of the Storm Regt. were gathered originally at HILDESHEIM and HALBERSTADT, but they completed their training at SENNE and BERGEN (near HANOVER). There is evidence that Gruppe 1 of Luftlandungs geschwader 1 is based at HILDESHEIM and that Gruppe II may possibly be based at HALBERSTADT or GOSLAR.

SECTION V

Their training, according to a captured ▓▓▓ and to a prisoner of war glider pilot, consisted in practice of loading and entering and leaving the aircraft with full equipment. A short flight was then made after which the glider was released and landed on the aerodrome. One P. of W. stated that in these practice flights 3 gliders at a time are sometimes towed. On landing, the glider troops deplaned and attacked, the pilot joining them. No details of these exercises are available, but it appears that elaborate practice manoeuvres were held involving inter-unit cooperation and the use of Ground strips and light signals for communication to aircraft, in addition to lessons in defensive circle formation.

One prisoner of war stated that ordinary infantry troops are carried in gliders, and that no special training is given. In view of the special nature of the tasks allotted to glider units, however, and to the concentrated fire power placed at their disposal, and also bearing in mind the small number of glider-borne troops employed, it would appear that this information was given either in ignorance or intentionally to mislead.

Previous Operational Experience.

Many of the glider pilots who operated in CRETE had already taken part in the BELGIAN and NORWEGIAN campaigns and had been decorated for their part in those actions. A prisoner of war from the present 1st Coy. Storm Regt. was decorated for a successful attack on a bridge over the Albert Canal in May, 1940. Another had been to NORWAY with a unit of 21 gliders, 15 of which ultimately returned.

D.F.S. 230 troop carrying Glider.

The glider used in the CRETE campaign was the D.F.S. (Deutsche Forschungsantalt fur Segelflugzeug) 230. This is a high winged 10 seater monoplane with a single fin and rudder, and monoplane tailplane and elevator. The length is about 50 feet, and the wing span about 80 feet.

The fuselage is of light tubular steel construction, the

SECTION V

wings of wood. The whole is fabric covered. Wheels are provided for the use on training flights, but on operational flights they are jettisoned and the landing is made on a skid.

No auxiliary engine is fitted.

Flying Instruments.

    Airspeed Indicator.   )
)
    Altimeter   ) These are illuminated
) by dashboard lamps.
    Turn and bank indicator)
)
    Compass)
)
    Rise and fall indicator)

Lighting and Electrical Equipment

Two aerial navigation lights are fitted for night flying. A landing light is placed under the port wing, and cabin and dashboard lamps are provided. The electrical equipment is worked by an accumulator stowed in the nose of the aircraft. No W/T., is carried.

Diving Brakes.

Flaps are fitted to upper trailing edge of wing, opening upwards to steepen angle of glide. When the flaps are closed during the glide, the nose does not drop suddenly as with power driven aircraft.

Assembly.

According to a P. of W. the 15 Gliders of his Staffel had their wings and flying wires rigged in one day at SALONIKA after having arrived by train. Each glider had one fitter and rigger.

Performance.

    Towing speed (with Ju.52.) - 105 mph.
    Optimum gliding speed. - 70 mph.
    Hold-off speed. - 55 mph.
    Landing Speed. - 35/40 mph.

SECTION V

Take-off run and Landing area.

The take-off run required is the normal take-off run of the Ju. 52 plus the length of the tow rope used and glider. Normally speaking a run of at least 800 yards is required. A longer run enables a longer tow rope to be employed.

The glider can be landed in any field or area where 20-50 yds. reasonably flat surface can be obtained. When short landings on smooth ground are required, barbed wire is sometimes wrapped around the skid.

Range after Cast-off

The following figures are taken from a captured report issued by the Government Testing Station at RECHLIN in March 1940. (The full report is given at the end of this Section).

D.F.S. 230.

Cast-off Height.	Head Wind Speed	Range
3,000 ft.	20 mph.	$7\frac{1}{2}$ miles
10,000 "	20 "	25 "
16,000 "	20 "	44 "
	Tail Wind Speed.	
3,000 ft.	20 mph.	$12\frac{1}{2}$ miles
10,000 "	20 "	44 "
16,000 "	20 "	75 "

Note: No provision has been made for oxygen to be carried. Heights above 10,000 ft. are therefore unlikely to be used.

Capacity.

The weight of the machine is 1716 lbs., and its maximum carrying capacity (pilot, passengers and goods) is 2900 lbs. This is made up in various ways according to the requirements in each particular case.

Seating accommodation is provided for 10 persons (1 pilot and 9 passengers) seated in single row one behind the other. Assuming an average weight of 140 lbs., per person, this gives a total of 1,400 lbs., and allows approximately as much weight again of equipment

SECTION V

to be carried.

The equipment is carried in the fore and rear compartments and under the seats. The last four seats are removable and the space can be used, if required, for equipment or supplies. In planning the loading of the glider, the weight of each man and his equipment is carefully noted. The loading is arranged so that the total weight carried is divided in certain proportions throughout the machine. In particular, the balance of weight fore and aft is carefully considered. One captured loading sheet indicates that the loading was arranged to give 800 kgs. fore and 450 kgs. aft of seats 6/7.

The weapons and ammunition carried by each section of three Gliders are to some extent complementary and are designed to be used together for the particular objective which it is proposed to attach, but as far as possible, each individual Glider is self-contained and carries very considerable fire power. This, one Glider carried four tommy-guns, with 48 magazines, ten pistols, 92 hand grenades and 12 kilos of explosives. Another Glider carried a light machine-gun with 3,000 rounds, 10 .08 pistols, 3 tommy-guns, 81 hand grenades, 9 rifles and 26 kilos of explosives.

Further details of actual equipment carried, as shown by captured documents in CRETE are given at the end of this section.

Armaments.

Sometimes an M.G. 34 (rifle bore) machine-gun is clamped outside the starboard side of Glider. This is operated through a slit (normally closed by zip fastener) and can only fire in the direction of flight. It is usually used mainly for moral effect just before landing.

Gliders do not carry any protecting armour.

Towing

In operational flights Ju. 52's are invariably employed. He. 46 and Hs .126 have sometimes been used in training flights.

Normally only one Glider is towed by each Ju. 52 though two may be towed, and prisoners of war state that as many as three

- 38 -

SECTION V

have been towed during training.

In the actual attacks on CRETE however, only one Glider was towed by each aircraft, and it is the general opinion of Glider Pilots that for operational purposes it is not practicable to tow more than one.

The length of cable is 40, 60, 80, 100, or 120 meters according to the aerodrome space available.

The towing cable is normally released by the Glider pilot, but, in emergency, may be released by towing aircraft. The release mechanism consists of a simple parrot beak hook.

When more than one Glider is towed, each aircraft is attached to a separate hook on the towing aircraft, as follows:-

Ju. 52.   Ju. 52.

Two Gliders.   Three Gliders.

The longer the cable the better the behaviour of the Glider in the air, but a long cable requires a correspondingly long take-off. One P. of W. in CRETE stated that they took off from TANAGRA. Owing to the limited space available the shortest tow rope (40 Metres) was used. As a result, they had a bumpy passage, and on approaching CRETE the tow rope broke. Cases also occurred of tow ropes snapping during a turn when the tow rope suddenly tightened after the turn.

Glider troops going over to GREECE, all carried gas masks and Losantin, and each man wore a life belt.

Glider-borne troops do not carry parachutists.

Only one pilot is carried in each Glider. There is no reserve Pilot and no observer. The pilot is given exact instructions regarding the point at which he is to land, and it is his duty to land the Glider as near as possible to that point. A captured hand-drawn sketch in CRETE showed by a red dotted line and arrow, the course to be taken by the Glider, and the exact point at which it was to land. (See Appendix "

SECTION V

The glider pilot is armed only with a .08 pistol. When he has landed the Glider he joins the other troops and takes part in the attack.

Ammunition and equipment, is stowed on both sides and beneath the seating, and in additional storage space fore and aft. The spare ammunition is stored in containers just behind the pilots seat, and a direct hit on this point may blow up the whole glider. At least one glider was destroyed in this way when descending in CRETE. Another was blown up intentionally by its crew.

SECTION V

Tactical

In CRETE gliders were used only in the first 15 minutes of the attack. They did not appear again.

Their arrival in the BALKANS had been a closely safeguarded secret, and the GERMANS believed that the attack would be a complete surprise. More than one prisoner of war was furious because he considered that the plan for the use of Gliders had leaked out through the GREEKS.

Gliders flew by platoons in sections of three, each Glider being towed separately by a Ju. 52. They maintained formation throughout the flight and attempted to land as near together as possible.

Fighter escort of Me. 109s and Me. 110s was provided on the final stage of the journey. A company of 15 gliders was given an escort of 12 Me. 109s and 6 Me. 110s, which were detailed to accompany them from KYTHERA ISLAND to the landing point on the AKROTIRI PENINSULA and give support until the first fighting was settled.

In all cases, objectives were bombed and machine-gunned prior to the arrival of the gliders. In the two places where the gliders were successful (MALEME and south of CANEA) the air attack continued all round the area while the gliders were landing and the actual landing was effected unperceived.

Many gliders crashed on landing. In one glider three of the occupants were killed, and four injured, leaving only three ready for action. In another, four of the occupants were killed, and the heavy machine-gun was broken in the crash. In a third case, the tow rope snapped before the glider had arrived at its destination. On landing, the glider broke its back, and the wings fell off, but the crew were only mildly shaken. They were immediately surrounded by GREEKS and taken prisoners. These crashes occurred on rough hard ground. On softer ground, they would not have happened.

On landing, the glider troops deplane as quickly as possible, carrying with them the weapons and tools they require for immediate use. Reserve ammunition and equipment was left in the glider until required. Each man carried with him a very considerable weight of ammunition, weapons and equipment.

SECTION V

Glider troops operated on platoons of three Gliders, each platoon being alloted a specific objective. In the case of one company (the Altmann Company) company orders giving detailed orders for each platoon were captured. One platoon was to occupy a specified A.A. battery, put the remaining guns in order ready for firing, obstruct the road just north of position and then support the attack of the second platoon on a group of houses, 1,000 metres west of the gun position. Similarly, the third and fourth platoons were to attack a specified gun position and groups of nearby houses in the same neighborhood. Finally, Headquarters Platoon was to land and take possession of the captured houses west of the battery position and cover Company Battle Headquarters from east, north and south.

Incidentally, the attack at this point was not a success. The ground was very rough and many of the gliders crashed on landing. Many of the troops were killed or wounded in the crash, the others were rapidly killed or captured by our troops. The glider troops in this area do not appear to have received air support on the same scale as in other sectors.

If opposition was met with on landing, the Glider troops formed themselves immediately into a defensive circle, taking advantage of any cover available from rough ground. A P. of W. from one Glider which crash landed stated that his Glider was wrecked on landing, the crew were momentarily dazed, and the P. of W. himself was winded, but none of them was badly hurt. They found themselves surrounded on three sides by machine-gun nests. To their amazement our men got out of their trenches and roared with laughter. Apparently they thought that all the Glider crew had been killed. However, the Glider crew disembarked, and formed a defensive circle, getting some cover from the bumpy ground. They held out for four hours, at the end of which they had all been killed except the prisoner of war and two other men who were wounded. The P. of W. said that he was amazed that our men did not use grenades or mortars. Had they done so the Glider crew would have been killed within a few minutes.

SECTION V

To Summarize:-

Tactically, gliders were employed for the following purposes:

1. To destroy A.A. gun positions in the line of approaching troop carrying aircraft.

2. To seize positions and give covering fire to the arrival of parachutists.

3. To cut communication, seize wireless stations, cut telephone lines.

4. To seize important personages.

5. To provide heavily armed storm troops for the capture of key points.

In every case, glider troops were used in the first wave of the attack. They preceded parachutists and prepared the way for them, just as parachutists frequently precede air landing troops.

The particular advantage of glider troops over parachutists is that glider-borne troops land complete with equipment and ready for immediate action, whereas the parachutist has to collect his equipment and form up with his comrades before they can take effective action. A further advantage is that they have more control over flight than parachutists, and, subject to ground conditions being suitable, can land at a given point, ex., alongside or behind a battery position, with considerable accuracy. This combination of concentrated fire power and spot landings allied to the element of surprise, proved to be most deadly in at least one case in CRETE. On the other hand, the glider is very vulnerable while in the air, and if the element of surprise is missing or if the terrain is unsuitable, the glider may be shot down or the troops put out of action before any action on their part is possible.

SECTION V

Captured Glider Loading Sheets

The "CZEWINSKI" Glider.

    Crew

              Pilot.
              Section Leader.
      ?   Deputy Section.
      ?   Rifleman.
      3   men-crew of light machine-gun.
      3   men-crew of light mortar.

    Equipment

      4   Tommy guns and 48 magazines.
      1   light machine gun with 2 drums and 8 boxes of amm: at 300 a box, and 1,200 rounds with No. 3 of crew = 3,600 and
      1   light mortar and 9 boxes ammunition
     10   Pistols
      2   Rifles with 200 rounds SS.
     12   Kilos balsting charge.
     92   Hand grenades.

      2   Spades.
      2   wire cutters.
      1   binoculars
      1   axe with claw
      1   set spare parts.

    Total weight, crew and equipment   =   1,285.4 kgs.

2. The "ORTH" Glider

    Crew

              Pilot.
              Section Leader.
              Troop Leader.
              Mortar Crew Leader.
      4   Riflemen
      1   M.G. Crew.

    Equipment

      1   M.G. 34 with boxes. Single & twin barrel containers, base plate, bipod, aiming posts, dial sight.
     15   Boxes heavy mortar ammunition
      9   .08 pistols - 18 magazines.
      5   Tommy guns - 30 magazines.
      1   Carbine and 1 rifle with telescopic sight and 200 rounds.
      3   Heavy calibre pistols (Kampf Pistols).
     30   Hand grenades.

      3   Pairs binoculars.
      8   short spades.
      1   long spade
      3   wire cutters.
      1   cutting saw
      1   Engineer's outfit (Pionier Gerat).
      1   axe with claw.
      2   tool kits.

    Total weight, crew and equipment   =   1,285.4 kgs.

SECTION V

3. The "NAGEL" Glider.

   "Stabsmaschine 2".

   Crew of 8 including:-

          Pilot.
          Deputy Leader.
          Heavy mortar leader.
      3 Riflemen.
      2 others.

   Equipment

      1 Heavy mortar with trolley and 19 boxes ammunition.
      3 Carbines.
      3 Tommy guns with 1,280 rounds.
      8 .08 pistols with 704 rounds.
     45 Egg grenades.
     35 Stick grenades.
      2 Explosive charges.

      3 Pairs binoculars.
      3 Marching compasses.
      7 Folding spades.
      8 Jackknives.
      5 Pocket torches.
      1 Axe with claw.
      1 First Aid knapsack.
      1 Bread bag with rations.

   Total weight, crew and equipment   =   1,266 kgs.

4. The "RUMMLER" Glider.

   Crew

          Pilot.
          Section Leader.
          Deputy Section Leader.
      3 Riflemen
      3 Crew of light M.G.
      1 Medical orderly.

   Equipment

      1 Light M.G. and 10 boxes of ammunition (3,000 rounds) with barrel container, barrel protector, tripod, 2 drums.
      3 Tommy guns and 960 rounds.
     10 Pistols and 880 rounds.
      6 Rifles (one with telescopic sight)
      4 Carbines and
      5 Bandoliers with 500 rounds.
     81 Hand grenades.
      7 Explosive charges.
      7 Flags.
      1 First Aid knapsack
      1 Field Dressing.

   Total weight, crew and equipment   =   1,132 kgs.

SECTION VI

PARACHUTISTS

Forces Employed

Parachutists employed in the attack on CRETE were drawn mainly from Fliegerkorps VII. Smaller numbers were probably also supplied by 5th Mountain Division and possibly also by 22nd Division and 6th Mountain Division, but these units are designed to provide air landing troops rather than parachutists and are therefore dealt with in the next section.

Fliegerdivision VII as employed in the CRETE operation consisted of one Storm Regt. of glider troops and the following parachute units:-

Parachute Regt. I

Parachute Regt. II

Parachute Regt. III

Parachute M.G. Battalion (3 companies)

Parachute A.A. M.G. Battalion (3 companies)

Parachute Anti-tank Unit (3 companies)

Parachute Artillery Battery (3 troops, each of 4 guns)

Parachute Pioneer Battalion.

Parachute Signals Unit

Parachute Motor-Cycle Battalion

Parachute Engineer Unit

Parachute Medical Unit

Parachute Supply Unit

It is interesting to note that in the original plan it was proposed to send the heavier units including parachute artillery battery, parachute anti-tank units, parachute A.A. artillery units, parachute motor cycle battalion, parachute machine gun battalion, by ship. Owing to our naval opposition, however, elements of these units had perforce to be carried by air.

Organization

The organization of parachute units is very flexible and the composition of units can be easily and rapidly varied in accordance

SECTION VI

with the operation which is beign undertaken.

For the CRETE operation, Parachute Regts. I, II, and III, together with ancilliary units were employed. The capture of CRETE represented a complete large scale parachute operation, calling for uniformly well armed forces over a considerable area, and the parachute units were reorganized to give approximately equal fire power throughout. With this object one platoon of each machine gun company was transferred to each rifle company and replaced by an equivalent number of riflemen.

Each parachute regiment is organized on the basis of 3 battalions; each battalion with four companies numbered consecutively as the 13th Infantry gun company and 14th anti-tank company.

Company strength as shown by captured company lists varied considerably; one company had 144 men shown on the company list; another had 240 17 22. Another company list showed 225 men, of which 27 were M.T. drivers and only 196 were parachutists.

A feature of parachute units is the abnormally high per cent of N.C.O's. One company of 144 men, in CRETE had 4 officers, one Warrant Officer, 128 N.C.O's and only 11 (soldaten) men.

Other captured loading lists practically every member of the company as an N.C.O.

Uniform

The familiar parachutist's uniform was worn, consisting of knickerbocker trousers, open neck tunic with wide pockets, leather belt with flat rectangular buckle, non-lacing boots with thick rubber soles and round steel helmet with narrow brim. When jumping, a loose grey-green combination type overall with short wide legs was worn over the tunic. Reports were received that parachutists landed in New Zealand uniform, but these proved to be incorrect. They probably originated from the fact that on the first day parachutists who had captured some Dominion troops prove their

SECTION VI

prisoners before them as a shield.

On the other hand, a clear indication that the wearing of foreign uniforms had been considered is given by a captured order in which it is specifically stated "British uniforms will not be worn." This would appear to show not only that the possibility of such action had been considered, but that British uniforms were actually in possession of some of the parachutists.

Equipment carried by Parachutists

It has been said that a parachutist has no less than 47 separate pockets and containers. Whether this is true or not has not yet been established, but it is certain that the battle equipment of parachute troops is very comprehensive, as the following captured order shows:-

SECTION VI

When going into action parachutists take   days rations with them. Special parachute rations (Sprungverpfegung) were carried in a special haversack. These are reported to have included biscuits, hard bread, chocolate, dates, sausage, dried fruits, Vitamin "C" tablets and cigarettes. A large water bottle full of water was also carried, and parachutists were ordered to drink the water sparingly and avoid drinking water in the Island as far as possible. Further food supplies were dropped as requested by the display of appropriate ground strips.

Dropped Equipment

Equipment in addition to that carried by the parachutist himself was dropped separately in small containers. The containers bore colored markings to indicate the section to which they belonged. They varied in size from approximately 2' x 1' to 6' x 4', or even larger. Bigger containers were fitted with wheels on which they could be hauled.

Small containers were dropped with a single parachute, but bigger containers were dropped with 2, 3 or even 4 parachutes. A prisoner of war has stated that sometimes the parachutes used for dropping containers were bigger than those used by parachutists. As a general rule the parachutes attached to containers were white in color, but containers carrying medical supplies had pink parachutes.

The number, size and contents of the containers varied with the type of company. A complete list of containers dropped by the 2nd Platoon of a machine gun section was captured and is given at the end of this section. Each container was marked with a distinguishing color and markings, and the list gave the contents and weight in each case. The weight varied from $76\frac{1}{2}$ Kgs. to 149 Kgs.

SECTION VI

Specimen contents are as follows:

    2 Machine pistols, 4 Machine pistol magazines (32 rds),

    2 Rifles - 5 rds heavy pointed Ammn, 2 cartridge belts,

    1 pick-axe, 1 long spade, 2 short spades, 1 wire cutter,

    1 Bangalore torpedo, 1 hacksaw, 4 handgrenade bags, 9 stick

    handgrenades, 14 egg bombs, 3 smoke bombs, 2 smoke candles,

    29 detonators, 7 smoke detonators, 2 smoke candle lighters.

Another container held:

    1 complete mortar, 1 folding spade, 1 hatchet, 1 long spade,

    1 pickaxe, 1 folding hatchet, 2 bandoliers, 3 parachute

    ration bags, 2 tent canvasses.

    40 mortar bombs.

    1 bandolier with 100 rds, heavy pointed Ammn., 368 rds

    pistol ammn.

    3 stick grenades, 2 smoke handgrenades, 6 egg grenades,

    1 Rifle 98K with 5 rds, heavy pointed.

Altogether 14 containers were dropped for the use of a parachute formation of about 40 men. Usually one container was dropped to each 4 men, but in some cases one container was dropped to 3 or even 2 men. Each section had its own container. The container was dropped with or immediately after the section, so that they could pick it up and make use of it with the shortest possible delay. In view of the fact that each container bore a mark indicating the particular section for which it was intended, it may be assumed that containers are not interchangeable, and that each section must use its own containers and no others. Reference in other captured documents is made of sections packing containers ready for use.

Containers 5 feet long and 2 feet in diameter dropped in the HERAKLION area contained spare parts and tools for motor transport, including spare parts for British and American types of trucks.

SECTION VI

It was reported that weapons dropped at MALEME included a number of heavy (80 mm.) mortars.

Very complete high grade medical equipment was dropped. The cases opened up to form complete operating units. It is reported that test tubes full of blood for transfusion were also dropped.

It is known that motorcycles were dropped by parachute and a fairly well substantiated report states that light cars were dropped. There is, however, no evidence that tanks, either light or heavy were dropped.

Tactical: Parachutists were embarked in JU-52's at TANAGRA, ELEUSIS, MENIDI, CORINTH and TOPOLIA airdromes. For the first wave of the attack, supplies were embarked the previous day and embarkation began at 0445 hours. The first wave of parachutists arrived over their objective in CRETE, some 200 miles distant, at 0815. In the Central Sector a parachute force consisting of a complete regiment and other units totalling approximately 2,500 parachutists were expected to drop in one hour. The aircraft carrying the first force were to return to Greece and bring the 2nd wave of parachutists during the afternoon. The time allowed for the return journey, loading and trip back to CRETE was 8 hours.

The number of parachutists carried in each aircraft varied according to the unit involved, but as a general rule, 12 parachutists and 4 containers were carried. Each container held equipment for a section of 3 men, and was thrown out at the same time as, or immediately after the section jumped. One captured loading sheet showed 12 aircraft, each carrying 12 parachutists. In another case the captured loading sheet showed 12 aircraft, each carrying 12 or 13 parachutists in addition to the pilot and observer. This was the loading list of 7th Company, 2nd Bn., Parachute Regt. I.

- 51 -

SECTION VI

When 13 parachutists were carried the last on the list was the "reserve." Reports from observers in CRETE stated that particularly in the later phases of the attack, as many as 18 or 20 parachutists were carried in one aircraft. It is not possible to confirm these reports which were based on visual observation, but it is of course possible that larger numbers were carried at this later stage in order to make up for the lack of sea transport. One thing, however, appears certain, the parachute regiments operating in the first wave of the attack did not exceed 12 parachutists per aircraft, and in the case of some of the heavier units only 8 parachutists were carried in each JU-52, the additional weight being made up by extra containers.

Company loading sheets show that troops were divided into sections, usually of 36 men, each section being carried by a "Kette" of 3 aircraft. A typical parachute company consisted of 144 troops divided into 4 sections each carried by one "Kette" of 3 JU-52's.

Every effort was made to maintain maximum fire power of units. One interesting example of this is a captured loading order for a platoon of an Artillery Battalion, consisting of 32 men, 3 guns and 3 machine guns. There was some doubt whether this platoon could have 3 or 4 transport aircraft, and the loading sheet gave alternative loads for them. If 4 aircraft were available, each aircraft was to carry 8 men together with guns and equipment. If only 3 aircraft were available, however, 8 men were to be left behind, but the full number of guns and machine guns were to be taken.

The aircraft departed in flights of 3. On arriving over their objective, the aircraft circled around, then flew at a height of 200-500 feet across the area where the parachutists were to land. Jumping was carried out in

SECTION VI

formation. The "Absetzer" (O.C. Jump), flying in the leading aircraft of the "Kette" showed a yellow flag 2 minutes before jumping as a sign to get ready. Half a minute before the jump he showed a red/white flag. When the target was reached he pulled in the red/white flag, which was the signal to jump. If he waved both flags across, this was the signal "Don't jump." At night signals could be given by colored torches, in which case red meant "Get ready," green meant "Ready to jump" and white meant "Jump."

In individual aircraft the signal to jump was given by the leader by sounding the klaxon. A wounded parachutist stated that 12 men left the aircraft in 9 seconds. Before jumping the parachutists attached the ring of their parachutes to a wire running along the length of the aircraft inside, and as they moved forward towards the door slid this ring along the wire. On jumping the ring actuates the opening of the parachute, which then opens automatically, the maximum drop before opening being 180 ft. (Casualties from failure of the parachute to open are estimated by a prisoner of war to be about 1%). Parachutists left the plane by the door on the left hand side of the aircraft; the door on the right hand side being used to throw out equipment containers, etc.

A certain proportion of the parachutists carried tommy guns and revolvers at the ready during their descent to provide covering fire for the arrival of their unit. Others carried handgrenades which they threw in the event of opposition being present in the area where they were about to land.

SECTION VI

As a general rule, parachutists had mottled green and brown parachutes, which rendered them inconspicuous on the ground, and could be used for camouflage of captured motor vehicles, etc. Equipment containers on the other hand, had white parachutes. In this case the parachute would serve as a distinguishing feature to help the troops to locate the spot where the container had fallen. Medical supplies had pink parachutes. One report was received to the effect that different units had different colors of parachutes in order to help them to assemble, but this report has not been confirmed and is discounted, if only for the reason that parachutists disengage themselves from their parachutes as soon as possible on reaching the ground.

SECTION VII

Air Borne Troops.

Units involved.

The following units are believed to have supplied air landing troops in the CRETE operation.

Elements of 5th Mountain Division comprising Nos. 85 and 100 Mountain Rifle Regiments and No. 95 Signals Unit.

Elements of 22nd Division comprising (probably) Nos. 16, 47 and 65 Infantry Regiments.

Elements of 6th Mountain Division comprising (probably) Nos. 141 and 143 Mountain Rifle Regiments.

Of the above Nos. 85 and 100 Mountain Rifle Regts. and 95 Signals Unit of the 5th Mountain Division were definitely allocated to the operation from the start and were placed under Fliegerkorps XI. A captured code list of units under Fliegerkorps XI for the CRETE operation includes these three units. It is believed that they were attached to Fliegerkorps XI for the purpose of this particular operation, but it is of interest to note that captured personnel of these units in CRETE had German Air Force pay books. On the other hand they retained their army numbers.

The part played by 22nd Division in the operation is still obscure. It is known that 22nd Division were in the Balkans at the time when the operation was being planned, and a captured document in CRETE which unfortunately was later lost indicated that Nos. 16, 47 and 65 Infantry Regiments were to take part in the attack on CRETE. (These three regiments provided air landing troops on the attack on Holland in May, 1940).

- 55 -

SECTION VII.

A prisoner of war has also confirmed that 22nd Division was to participate in the attack. On the other hand, there is no record in captured documents or from other sources of the actual part played by any of these units in the operation. It is true of course that few documents were captured in the later phases of the attack, and that our knowledge of the forces engaged at that time is incomplete. It would appear probable that elements of those three regiments were among the troops ferried over by air to MALEME between May 23rd and May 29th.

6th Mountain Division was originally intended, so far as can be ascertained, to be employed in the CRETE operation, but there is evidence that Nos. 141 and 143 Mountain Rifle Regts, together with (probably) ancilliary units of the 6th Mountain Division were engaged in the later phases of the operation, and it may be concluded that in view of the unexpected strength of our resistance, those units were added as reinforcements. They stayed in CRETE only just long enough to complete the operation, after which they returned to GREECE. By the middle of June they were already on their way to the RUSSIAN frontier.

100 Mountain Rifle Regiment was to land at MALEME, and 85 Mountain Rifle Regiment at HERAKLION. It was originally intended to send heavier elements of these two regiments including Artillery and Anti-Tank Units, A.V.S. and M.T. by sea, the other units to be ferried over by air. So far as can be ascertained, it was not intended to drop large numbers of troops from these units by parachute. Their function was to provide air landing and sea-borne troops to follow the parachutists, who, in the meantime, were expected to have captured airdromes and landing areas. It is known, however, that a certain number of troops of these units have had training in parachute jumping, and ther could be, and possibly were, employed as parachutists. The bulk of the

Section VII.

forces, however, were ultimately landed by troop-carrying aircraft, chiefly at MALEME.

On the first morning of the attack, even before the airdrome at MALEME had been captured, two companies of air-landing troops believed to belong to 100 Mountain Rifle Regiment, were landed on the beaches at MALEME in the teeth of opposition. It is probable that these troops were sent off at a predetermined time after the first wave of parachutists with the intention of landing on the airdrome, and that when it was realized that the airdrome was still in our hands, they were crash landed, regardless of risk, at the nearest suitable point, which in this case happened to be the beaches east and west of the airdrome. A number of the aircraft crashed, and considerable casualties were caused among the troops both by crashes and by our fire, but some of the troops were able to disembark and take up positions.

During the afternoon, despite the fact that the airdrome was still partly in our hands, aircraft began to land with troops on the western side of the landing ground where they could get some covering fire from their troops established on the western fringe of the airdrome. This landing must have been an extremely hazardous operation, as the incoming aircraft were well within range of our Artillery and even small arms fire. "From a distance," reports one observer, "It appeared as if they were sailing into certain death." In the meantime, however, our troops and batteries were under constant bombing, dive bombing and ground straffing attacks from the enemy air forces, and this air support enabled the landing to be made, though considerable casualties are believed to have been inflicted. It is estimated that during this afternoon, three battalions of troops were landed by air at MALEME.

Section VII.

Using the reinforcement, thus received, and supported, as always, from the air, the GERMANS brought increasing pressure to bear against our forces to the east of the airdrome, and just before dusk we were compelled to evacuate the airdrome. A counter-attack during the night had some measure of success, but at dawn the following morning our troops were attacked from the air before they were able to dig in. This was followed by an enemy counter-attack which drove back our forces to a ridge some two miles east of the airdrome. This gave the GERMANS full use of the airdrome, though it was still under fire from our Artillery, and, at extreme range, from small arms. In spite of this, GERMAN troop-carrying aircraft began to arrive during the morning and continued to arrive throughout the day.

The troop-carrying aircraft arrived in groups of three, and were obviously timed to follow each other at short intervals so that a continuous stream was maintained. 3 or 4 personnel already on the spot, rushed to the aircraft and helped to unload it, and aircraft left with very little delay. Timed over a period of one day, aircraft landed and took off at an average rate of 12 per hour. When three aircraft landed together, two of them took off again very shortly afterwards, the third leaving about 10 - 12 minutes later. It appears probable that the third aircraft carried heavier equipment which was unloaded by the personnel who had been disembarked from the first two aircraft. In this way each section could be landed complete with both heavy and light equipment with a minimum of delay, and a maximum of concentration.

The transport aircraft landed and took off in an incredibly short space, estimated by observers at 400 - 500 yds. They returned to their bases singly, proceeding at a low height on a course parallel to that of the incoming

Section VII.

aircraft. The effect, according to observers, was that of a continuous moving band, and the sight of this constant stream of aircraft bringing in enemy reinforcements was most demoralizing to our troops.

Little or no fighter protection was provided, presumably in view of the fact that for some days at least there was no fighter opposition, but continuous reconnaissance was maintained overhead, and non-stop bombing and machine gun attacks on our troops and positions. In particular enemy air forces methodically located and destroyed our batteries firing on the airdrome and incoming aircraft.

APPENDIX NO. 4

Appendix No. 4   Services Committee on Crete

Pages 60-133

SERVICES COMMITTEE ON THE

CAMPAIGN IN CRETE

CONTENTS

OPENING REMARKS

	Page
Period covered by the Report	1
Arrangement of the Report...	1
The Background..	1
CRETE...	1

PART I

THE PREPARATORY PERIOD

(1st November, 1940, to 28th April, 1941.)

Outline of Events...	2 – 4
The Naval Aspect	4
The Air Aspect..	4

    Opening remarks 4
    Aerodromes............................... 5
    Aircraft pens............................ 5
    Petrol and Ammunition stocks............. 5
    Intercommunication....................... 5
    Operations Room Staff.................... 6
    Evacuation from GREECE................... 6
    Fighter protection....................... 7

PART II

THE PERIOD IMMEDIATELY PRECEDING THE ATTACK

(30th April to 19th May, 1941.)

Preparations for Defence, and Dispositions..	8 – 13
The Naval Aspect	13
The Air Aspect..	14

PART III

THE ATTACK AND EVACUATION

(30th May to 31st May, 1941)

The Fighting on May 20th	15 – 17

    MALEME sector........................... 15
    SUDA BAY sector......................... 16
    HERAKLION sector........................ 17
    RETIMO sector........................... 17
    The Royal Navy and the Royal Air Force
    take part in the land fighting.......... 17

The German Plan	18

Continuation of the fighting in the MALEME
    and SUDA BAY AREAS   19

General Freyburg moves his Headquarters...   20

General WESTON appointed to command all
    forces in the SUDA-CANEA area   20

The Critical 26th of May..   21

The Withdrawal from the SUDA-CANEA area to SPHAKIA   23

        The Decision to withdraw......................   23
        Difficulties of command.......................   23
        Withdrawal to the "Saucer"....................   23
        Withdrawal from the "Saucer" to
            Shakia and Evacuation.....................   24

Events at HERAKLION...   26

Events at RETIMO..   28

The Naval Aspect..   28

The Air Aspect   30

PART IV

SUMMARY OF LESSONS

<u>GENERAL REMARKS</u>...   32

        Ambiguity as to the role of Garrison..........   32
        Failure to prepare defences...................   33
        The Air Factor................................   34
        Enemy air action and the Supply Problem.......   34
        Problem of Fighter Aircraft...................   35
        Intercommunication............................   35
        Discipline and Morale.........................   35

Army Lessons

Defence against Glider borne attack and parachutists

        Enemy tactics.................................   36
        General measures recommended to meet
            such attacks..............................   36
        The Immediate Counter Attack..................   37
        Use of Light Tanks............................   37

Defence of Aerodromes.   37

Field Works...   38

Camouflage   39

Anti-Aircraft Defence.   39

Night Operations..   40

Artillery   40

Lack of Transport.   41

(iii)

Evacuation	41
Need for decentralization...........................	41
Necessity for early organization of beaches.......	41
Need for fresh troops to form bridgehead..........	41
Intercommunication between beach and assembly area	41
Necessity for cordon on beach......................	42

Naval Lessons

Docks Organization	42
Port Control Committee.............................	42
Hiding of light craft..............................	43
Merchant shipping crews............................	43
Evacuation	43
Beach organization.................................	43
Number to be embarked..............................	43
Camouflage	43
Various...	44
Discharge of portable cargo........................	44

Royal Air Force Lessons

Aerodromes	44
Reconnaissance and Selection.......................	44
Demolitions..	44
Construction and design of L.Gs....................	45
Obstruction of ground suitable for use by aircraft	45
Petrol and ammunition dumps........................	46
Protection of aircraft on the ground...............	46
Aerodrome defence..................................	46
Royal Air Force Uniforms..	46
Lessons learnt from Germans...	47
Introduction.......................................	47
Enemy air force....................................	47
Direction of enemy low flying aircraft.............	48
Provision of landing grounds.......................	48
Attacks on A.A. gun positions......................	49
Size of bombs......................................	49
Screaming bombs....................................	49
Supply dropping....................................	50
Gliders..	50
Parachutists.......................................	50
Employment of troop carrying aircraft..............	51
CONCLUDING REMARKS	52

A P P E N D I C E S

Appendix "A" – Administrative Narrative and Lessons

Appendix "B" – Order of Battle

Appendix "C" – Coast Defence and Anti-Aircraft Artillery

M A P S

Map 1 – CRETE

Map 1A– AREA SUDA-MALEME

Map 2 – Dispositions New Zealand Division a.m. 20/May

Map 3 – General WESTON'S Dispositions a.m. 26th May

Map 4 – Dispositions HERAKLION a.m. 20th May

Map 4A– Dispositions RETIMO a.m. 20th May

Map 5 – Withdrawal to SPHAKIA

OPENING REMARKS

PERIOD COVERED BY THE REPORT

1. This Report covers the period from 1st November, 1940, until 31st May, 1941.

ARRANGEMENT OF THE REPORT

2. The Report will be divided into four parts as under:-

    Part I   - The Preparatory Period
                (1st November, 1940, to 29th April, 1941.)
    Part II   - The period immediately preceding the
                attack. (30th April to 19th May, 1941.)
    Part III - The attack and evacuation
                (20th May to 31st May, 1941.)
    Part IV   - Summary of Lessons

An administrative narrative and lessons will be found at Appendix "A".

THE BACKGROUND

3. In order fully to understand the account of the fighting, the disadvantages under which the defenders were labouring should be stressed at the outset. Enemy air superiority was complete. If casualties were not always heavy, bombing and machine gunning were almost continuous throughout the day. Movement was limited to an extent unknown before. Meanwhile, wave after wave of aircraft continued unmolested and within sight of our troops to bring reinforcements to the enemy. Furthermore, the greater part of the garrison had taken part in the withdrawal from GREECE. Battalions were battalions in name only; they were weak in numbers; they had little signal equipment, little or no transport, few tools, and no cooking utensils; bully beef and cigarette tins replaced plates and mugs. These factors had a cumulative effect on morale and the measure of the resistance offered should be judged thereby. In contrast to this, on the other side of the hill, the enemy was free to move as he wished, while his heart was continually gladdened by the sight of his own aircraft.

4. The Greek battalions were but raw recruits with a few weeks training. Some had just been issued with modern weapons. That they should have been able to face the onslaught at all will redound to their undying credit.

CRETE (Map 1.)

5. Map 1 shows the physical features of the island. The main points to note are:-

    (a) In the main the island forms a continuous mountain range from east to west.
    (b) Roads are few. One skirts the northern coast. There are others linking this to the south coast from CANEA to SPHAKIA, RETIMO to PLAKA BAY, and HERAKLION to TYMBAKI.
    (c) Landing grounds for aircraft are few, but the MESSARA PLAIN offers facilities in an area about 14 miles by 2 miles.
    (d) The length of the coast line and the number of possible landing beaches complicate the defence problem.

PART I.

THE PREPARATORY PERIOD
(1st November, 1940, to 28th April, 1941)

1. The task given to Brigadier TIDBURY, the first British commander in CRETE, was to defend the Royal Naval refuelling base at SUDA BAY and, in co-operation with local Greek forces, to prevent and defeat any attempt by a hostile force to gain a foothold in the island.

2. At the outset, the forces placed at Brigadier TIDBURY'S disposal amounted to a brigade group (less two battalions). In addition, there was on the island the Cretan Division, and it was hoped that this would remain to participate in its defence.

3. At this time there was little reason to believe that a serious attack was imminent. Brigadier TIDBURY, however, in his first appreciation, did envisage the possibility of an eventual attack on a large scale, including airborne attempts against HERAKLION, RETIMO and CANEA. He therefore urged an intensive night and day digging programme with a view to strengthening the defences of the island. From the evidence available, this appears to be the only serious effort that was made to tackle the task in hand and it is to be regretted that his example was not followed.

4. Towards the Middle of November, owing to the situation in ALBANIA becoming serious, the Greek Commander in Chief urgently requested that the Cretan Division might be despatched to the mainland. This materially affected the capacity of the island to resist, but although the Commander in Chief Middle East opposed the request, he had eventually to agree. Three Greek battalions were, however, left behind and the Greek General Staff agreed to raise a reserve division, requesting us to provide the equipment. The provision of complete equipment was, of course, impossible, but it was agreed that 10,000 rifles should be provided.

5. The Commander in Chief Middle East at this time already had in mind the possibility of a division being required for the defence of the Naval and Air base in CRETE in the event of GREECE being overrun, and on the 24th of November the Officer Commanding the troops in CRETE was instructed to prepare a base to receive and maintain one division. He was also informed that the allotment of anti-aircraft artillery would ultimately be increased. The basic garrison of CRETE was to be one infantry brigade headquarters, two British infantry battalions, two British Commandos, four Greek battalions, seven heavy A.A. batteries and six light A.A. batteries. A plan was to be put in hand to reinforce the island with one division if necessary. No defence scheme, however, for the defence of the island by one British division would appear to have been drawn up.

6. At the beginning of April, after British Forces had moved to GREECE, the importance of CRETE increased and it was decided to develop SUDA BAY as a Fleet Base as opposed to a refuelling base. It was therefore decided to send the M.N.B.D.O. to CRETE.

7.   Meanwhile there had been a frequent change of command in the island and there was some ambiguity as to what the defence plans should be. No less than fiv commanders were appointed within a period of six months. General GAMBIER-PARRY had succeeded Brigadier TIDBURY; Brigadier GALLOWAY, who succeeded General GAMBIER-PARRY, was instructed to be responsible for the defence of SUDA BAY only. It will be noted that these instructions conflicted with those given to the first commander. At the end of March, Brigadier CHAPPELL succeeded Brigadier GALLOWAY and immediately pointed out that he was in some doubt as to what defence plan was intended. He realised that the garrison might eventually be increased to one division but he did not understand whether he was to make plans for the defence of the limited area which included RETIMO, SUDA and CANEA, or whether the division was to be split up into brigade groups and to include in its task the defence of HERAKLION.

8.   Towards the end of April, Major General Weston, Royal Marines, Commanding M.N.B.D.O., was sent out to CRETE with instructions to make a report. He appreciated that he had to contend with two possible sets of circumstances, viz.,

   (a) those obtaining at the time he arrived when he considered his main object to be the security of the Fleet base, and

   (b) those that would obtain if the situation on the mainland deteriorated and a serious attack on Crete became imminent.

In the latter eventuality he appreciated that his task would include the defence of the island against invasion.

9.   General WESTON thought it necessary to consider the defence of the important areas of SUDA BAY and HERAKLION as separate and self-contained problems. He also pointed out the inadequate harbour facilities at SUDA BAY and stated his intention of developing HERAKLION.

10.   With regard to the possible scale of enemy attack, General WESTON appreciated that the enemy might disembark a lightly equipped brigade of approximately 3,000 men covered by the necessary air support including parachutists at either or both ends of the island, or at RETIMO. To meet this threat he considered that an infantry brigade group with a detachment at RETIMO would be required to secure HERAKLION and that another infantry brigade group would be required for the area SUDA - MALEME. If Greek troops were available, they were to be primarily responsible for the defence of the eastern end of CRETE which would become another self-contained area. He considered also that they might be of use in the defence of the area RETIMO.

11.   The General, in his appreciation, envisaged the location of fighter and bomber aircraft in the island and he favoured the construction of further full scale operational aerodromes provided their location was related to the limitations of ground defence and available troops.

12.   Finally, General WESTON proposed that on the arrival of M.N.B.D.O., Headquarters 14 Infantry Brigade should be separated from Headquarters GREFORCE which would comprise his own headquarters. The Brigade should be separately organized and be prepared to operate as a Brigade Headquarters in the field. The Brigade should also have

additional responsibilities for Army defence throughout the island, such as reconnaissance for the dispositions of the division on arrival and co-operation with the Greek military authorities. On the arrival of the HERAKLION Brigade Commander, the latter would take over responsibilities in respect of that area.

13.   Shortly after General WESTON'S appreciation had been written, it was decided to evacuate GREECE. General WESTON was therefore ordered to be prepared to receive about 25,000 evacuees and he arranged reception areas in the following three localities:-

        (a)   East of SUDA POINT
        (b)   Area CANEA
        (c)   Area 9 miles west of CANEA

THE NAVAL ASPECT

14.   Many of the naval questions are covered by the Administrative Narrative and Lessons at Appendix "A".

15.   The defences of SUDA BAY against seaborne attack were brought up to the standard required for the scale laid down by the Joint Planning staff and during this period the harbour was used as an advanced fuelling base for the Fleet. Lighters for the disembarkation of large quantities of stores were not made available as there was no immediate need, but there were at all times adequate facilities for the comparatively small quantity of stores and equipment to be disembarked. During the next phase when the "Eleventh hour supply rush" commenced, sufficient lighters were quickly made available by using some of the "A" lighters, M.L.C.s and A.L.C.s which had been used for the evacuation of GREECE.

THE AIR ASPECT

16.   During this phase no Royal Air Force operational units were located permanently in CRETE until the evacuation of GREECE began. The Fleet Air Arm maintained a fighter squadron, No. 805, at MALEME for the defence of the Fleet anchorage at SUDA BAY, and the Royal Air Force used SUDA BAY as an advanced base for the flying boats of No. 230 Squadron.

17.   In December, 1940, No. 252 A.M.E.S. was established at MALEME as part of the defence system for SUDA BAY, but until April of 1941, the Royal Air Force was chiefly concerned with administrative problems. These were principally the improvement and construction of aerodromes and the building up of petrol, bomb and ammunition stocks.

18.   Soon after the occupation of the island a Flight Lieutenant was appointed first Senior Air Force Officer CRETE. His duties were to supervise and watch over Royal Air Force interests on the island and to act as immediate air advisor to the General Officer Commanding CRETE. In view of the seniority and experience of these officers it is considered that the instructions issued to them were inadequate. Royal Air Force interests in CRETE were not clearly defined, and the officers appear to have been given no guide regarding air policy or requirements. In consequence these Senior Air Force Officers could be of little use as advisors and the manner in which they were able to watch over air force interests depended largely upon individual imagination and initiative.

Aerodromes

19. The principal task undertaken during the period of occupation was the improvement of existing aerodrome facilities at HERAKLION and the construction of additional aerodromes at MALEME and RETIMO, PEDIADA, KASTELLI, MESSARA PLAIN and KASSAMOS KASTELLI.

20. Shortage of constructional equipment, tools, and particularly of lorries, reduced the rate at which work was done. The fact that only one Works Directorate engineer was available to supervise the working parties was an additional handicap.

21. When the offensive began only MALEME, RETIMO and HERAKLION were virtually completed. The landing ground at PEDIADA KASTELLI had been partially completed, but on the 12th of May the G.O.C. CRETE decided that his force was insufficient to provide protection for it. The work was abandoned and the site permanently obstructed.

22. Little effort appears to have been made to find or construct satellite landing grounds for MALEME, RETIMO or HERAKLION. That provision of such landing grounds was possible was shown by Group Captain G. R. BEAMISH within a few days of his arrival on the island on 17th April, as S.A.F.O. He at once found a suitable site at DERES some 5 miles south east of MALEME. This site was never developed because it represented an additional defence commitment for the garrison. Similarly it is considered that dispersion of aircraft at the completed aerodromes would have been improved by the construction of tracks leading off them, although this might have further complicated the question of anti-aircraft defence.

Aircraft Pens

23. On the 17th April the only pens which had been constructed were at HERAKLION. These had been designed for Wellington aircraft and were modified to accommodate two fighters. By this means, and by additional construction, nine pens were ready for use when the offensive began. At the same date no pens were available either at MALEME or RETIMO. Construction at MALEME was initiated by Group Captain BEAMISH, and at RETIMO arrangements were made to hide aircraft in the adjacent olive groves owing to the lack of suitable building material.

24. It is considered that construction of these pens should have been undertaken concurrently with the other work done on the landing grounds. Protection for aircraft would then have been available immediately the aerodromes were fit for use. The Committee are of opinion that much more could have been done if this policy of construction had been adopted from the start.

Petrol, Bomb, and Ammunition Stocks

25. Adequate stocks were despatched to CRETE before the German attack began. Their disposition, however, was left largely to the discretion of S.A.F.O. CRETE, and it is considered that instructions in this respect should have been issued by Headquarters, Royal Air Force, Middle East. At HERAKLION the fact that these were sited outside the defence perimeter indicates a singular lack of initiative on the part of the Royal Air and Military commanders.

26. At MALEME some confusion arose over the question of providing units of the Fleet Air Arm with petrol. They were in fact supplied from Royal Air Force sources, the most economical method of doing it - but the requirements of the two Services were not well co-ordinated and might have resulted in shortage of petrol, etc. In order to remove any doubt regarding the supply of petrol and bombs, a definite policy concerning their provision, at times when units from both Services are using the same aerodrome, should be laid down.

Inter-communication

27. Little was done to improve telephone communications during the period of occupation and this is examined in full detail in Appendix "A". Communications between the aerodromes operations rooms and the A.M.E.S. was all done by a single cable. Operationally these became useless as soon as the attack developed, and the value of the A.M.E.S. nullified. It is clear that if A.M.E.S. are to be of any value, sufficient lines must be laid to ensure that the information they obtain can be passed with a high degree of certainty. The efficiency and value of both fighter and anti-aircraft defences depends largely upon the warnings given by these stations. Therefore, the provision of adequate and protected telephone lines between A.M.E.S. and operation rooms must be given very high priority in any future system of defence.

28. Royal Air Force arrangements for point to point W/T communication were satisfactory, the main station being at HERAKLION.

Operations Room Staff

29. Although No. 252 A.M.E.S. was established on the island in December, 1940, no proper operations room staff was provided at CANEA. In fact the operations room staff for No. 252 A.M.E.S. and No. 220 A.M.E.S. at HERAKLION were only completed between 18th and 25th April, from personnel evacuated from GREECE. The efficiency of an operations room depends upon team work, and this cannot be obtained without practice. It is considered that the staff at CANEA should have been placed on an operational basis as soon as No. 252 A.M.E.S. had been properly established, and certainly not later than the entry of Germany into GREECE.

Evacuation from GREECE

30. With the evacuation of GREECE, CRETE at once became an active operational base. The duties of S.A.F.O. CRETE were taken over by Group Captain G.R. BEAMISH on the 17th of April and he established his Headquarters at CANEA.

31. The main tasks undertaken during the ensuing period were the provision of fighter protection for convoys to and from GREECE and the reception and transfer to EGYPT of Royal Air Force personnel arriving from GREECE. In addition a W/T station had to be established at CANEA.

32. The evacuation of personnel from GREECE to CRETE and later to EGYPT was assisted by No. 230 Squadron operating from SUDA BAY, and bomber transport aircraft from HERAKLION.

Fighter Protection

33.   In the vicinity of GREECE, convoy protection was provided by Blenheim aircraft operating in patrols of six. On approaching CRETE and during disembarkation at SUDA BAY convoys were covered by fighter aircraft. As far as possible all convoys were provided with a measure of protection during daylight.

34.   Most of the protection was provided by remnants of those units which had flown to CRETE from GREECE. These were supported by No. 203 Squadron from EGYPT, which was the only squadron not in a low state of serviceability. In fact, on the 24th April, although three squadrons of Blenheims and two squadrons of fighters were in CRETE, the number of serviceable aircraft was no more than fifteen Blenheims and twelve fighters.

35.   The evacuation from GREECE continued from 21st to 29th April and fighter escorts were provided throughout the period. On the 30th April/1st May No. 203 Squadron returned to EGYPT and the units then left in CRETE were No. 30 Squadron at MALEME, Nos. 33 and 80 Squadrons at MALEME, No. 112 Squadron at HERAKLION, and No. 805 (F.A.A.) squadron at MALEME. The combined strengths of these units now amounted to 36 aircraft, but operationally only half that number were fit for use.

Page ... 8

PART II

THE PERIOD IMMEDIATELY PRECEDING THE ATTACK

(30th April to 19th May, 1941.)

1. On the 28th of April, General WILSON reached CRETE from GREECE and submitted an appreciation in which he pointed out that it would not be difficult for the enemy to launch a seaborne attack as he would be able to provide air protection for it, and that it would be difficult for the Royal Navy seriously to interfere. The distance was short, forces could be landed in twelve hours and ships withdrawn. When the Fleet arrived it would be attacked with the maximum concentration of aircraft and as soon as it retired, as eventually it must, the enemy would be able to land reserves of ammunition and stores. There would be little subsequent chance of the Fleet interfering and the enemy had unlimited forces with which to follow up the landing. Meanwhile few reinforcements would be able to be sent to the British garrison in CRETE.

2. General WILSON recommended that the HERAKLION and CANEA areas should be held at all costs since each had one aerodrome the loss of which would seriously jeopardise subsequent relief if German forces landed in the island. He considered that the minimum force required would be three brigade groups each of four battalions, and one motor battalion. This was over and above the M.N.B.D.O. required for the defence of SUDA. He also urged air protection for vital points and that further anti-aircraft artillery was necessary. He concluded by expressing the belief that unless the three Services were prepared to face the situation and maintain adequate forces up to strength, the holding of the island was a dangerous commitment and he asked for an immediate decision.

3. Meanwhile, instructions were received that the island should be denied to the enemy, but it was pointed out that the Royal Air Force would be able to send no reinforcements for some time.

4. At this juncture Major General FREYBURG was appointed Commander-in-Chief of the Graeco-British Forces in CRETE. Warning had already been received from Middle East that an airborne attack was imminent and that it might be carried out by a German air division, a German mountain division and an Italian infantry division. This warning was repeated on the 29th and the scale of possible attack mentioned as being in the neighbourhood of 3,000 or 4,000 parachutists in the first flight. General Freyburg protested that he had insufficient forces with which to meet the scale of attack mentioned. Furthermore they were ill equipped. He urged that fighter aircraft be greatly increased and that naval forces be made available to deal with seaborne attack. He concluded by saying that he would fight, but gave out no hope of being able to repel invasion. If the aircraft he demanded could not be made available, he requested that the decision to hold CRETE should be reconsidered. The Commander-in-Chief replied that although the possible scale of attack might have been exaggerated, serious attack was nevertheless likely. Although the situation as regards fighter aircraft was difficult, every effort was being made to acquire reinforcements from home. He fully appreciated General FREYBURG'S difficult situation but was confident that his troops would be equal to the task.

Page ... 9

5. Before the arrival of troops evacuated from GREECE, the garrison of CRETE consisted of:

    14th Infantry Brigade
    The greater part of M.N.B.D.O.
    The anti-aircraft and coast defence artillery

Troops reaching the island from GREECE included:

    4th New Zealand Brigade
    5th New Zealand Brigade
    19th Australian Brigade (which included parts of
      five Australian battalions.)
    A mixed party of British troops including gunners and
      others without their equipment.

The state of these troops was stressed at the beginning of this Report and should be again mentioned.

6. In accordance with arrangements already made by General WESTON, the above troops on arrival were located in three areas as under:

    Australians   - East of SUDA
    British   - In area SUDA - CANEA
    New Zealanders - In area about five miles west of CANEA.

7. In addition, there were on the island three Greek garrison battalions comprising reservists and partly fit men, and eight recruit battalions composed of men with anything from one week to one month's training. These troops were equipped with no less than five different types of rifle and, on an average, thirty rounds of ammunition per rifle only were available. Brigadier SALISBURY-JONES was instructed to assist in their re-organization. Although hardly in a position to face a modern European army, every effort was made to fit this force for a defensive role and British and Imperial officers were attached to each battalion.

8. General FREYBURG'S plan was to dispose his troops into four self-contained sectors as under:

    <u>HERAKLION</u>   Commander - Brigadier CHAPPELL,
                        Commanding 14th Infantry Brigade.

              2nd Black Watch
                2nd Yorks and Lancs.
                300 of 1 Australian Battalion
                250 of 7 Medium Regiment R.A. armed as infantry.
                Three Greek battalions.

    <u>RETIMO</u>   Commander - Brigadier VASEY, Commanding 19th
                  Australian Brigade.

              Two Australian and three Greek battalions holding
                the aerodrome
              Two battalions at GEORGOPOULIS.
              One battalion area STYLOS.
              Some Greek troops and police at RETIMO.

Page ... 10

    SUDA BAY   Commander - Major General WESTON, commanding SUDA BAY sector.

                        Northumberland Hussars (100 rifles).
                        106 R.H.A. (improvised rifle battalion).
                        1st Rangers (400 rifles).
                        700 rifles PERVOLIA Transit Camp.
                          (known as "Royal Perivolians" composed of details of various British units).
                        16 and 17 Infantry Brigades (very weak).
                        Two Greek battalions.
                        Personnel of base installations, etc.

    MALEME.   Commander - Brigadier PUTTICK, commanding New Zealand Division

                        4 New Zealand Brigade in area 3 miles west of CANEA.
                        5 New Zealand Brigade in area MALEME.
                        Three Greek battalions.

9.   As regards air forces in the island, the Air Officer Commanding in Chief had informed Group Captain BEAMISH on the 24th of April that he proposed to retain one Blenheim fighter squadron for convoy duties in the SUDA area, to build up one fighter squadron the same area, and to keep one fighter squadron for the time being at HERAKLION. In spite of the lack of preparation for protecting and concealing aircraft, it was apparently hoped at this stage that notwithstanding enemy air superiority these squadrons would survive.

10.   Feverish preparations were now put in hand, but the defenders were severely handicapped by lack of tools and transport. Much was sent from EGYPT during this period, including Italian and various other types of guns. Much, however, was sunk. Colonel FREWIN, C.R.A. for the New Zealand Division, wasted no time in organizing instruction and when the attack started all guns were capably manned. A brief account of the defence measures taken in each sector is given below.

HERAKLION SECTOR (Map 4)

11.   The problem was to protect the town and harbour of HERAKLION, the aerodrome which lay about three miles to the east of the town, and the beach on which seaborne landings or crash landings by aircraft might be attempted.

12.   Ten Bofors guns of which six were static and four mobile were located around the aerodrome. Two sections each of two field guns were sited to the west and southwest of the aerodrome to cover the aerodrome and harbour. Two companies of the Black Watch, with one platoon and a section of carriers dug in, were located for the close defence of the aerodrome. Two 'I' tanks were also concealed nearby. The remainder of the Black Watch were dug in covering level ground adjacent to the aerodrome, and one company was given a counterattack role. Nine 100 mm and four 75 mm guns, together with six light tanks were located southwest of the aerodrome.

13.   The remainder of the brigade occupied areas facing outwards

about 2,000 yards from the aerodrome. The town was defended by one trained Greek battalion and two battalions of Greek recruits.

14. The Brigade Commander imposed no restrictions on opening fire by A.A. guns but all else was to be concealed until the preliminary bombardment was over. Each unit was made responsible for immediate counterattack against parachutists in its own area. Tanks and reserves as ordered by the Brigade Commander were to emerge and deal with parachute landings and troop carriers. The field guns were not to open fire on the aerodrome until ordered. The intention of the Brigade Commander was to give this order only if troop carriers landed in numbers or the anti-aircraft guns were knocked out.

15. Rations for five days were issued to each unit and detachments were told to hold water on the scale of one gallon a day for six days.

RETIMO SECTOR   4a).

16. At RETIMO there were two problems:

    a. the defence of the RETIMO area proper, which included the defence of the town and harbour, the aerodrome and a stretch of beach to the east upon which sea landings might take place or crashed aircraft land, and

    b. the prevention of a seaborne landing in the area GEORGOPOULIS.

Brigadier VASEY therefore allotted two Australian battalions and two Greek battalions for the defence of RETIMO and the aerodrome, and two Australian battalions for the defence of the GEORGOPOULIS beaches. Similar dispositions for the protection of the aerodrome were taken up as in the case of the aerodrome at HERAKLION. A few Greek reservists only were in RETIMO.

SUDA BAY SECTOR

17. The problem at SUDA BAY was to protect the harbour and base installations in the area CANEA. Two Australian battalions were located east of SUDA POINT with a view to preventing any enemy advance on SUDA from the east. A general line was also taken up south of CANEA to prevent any enemy parachute troops who might land in the olive groves south of that area advancing into CANEA. Finally, a detachment was located on the peninsular with a view to preventing any parachutists landing in that area advancing across the neck of the peninsular into CANEA and the area occupied by Force Headquarters.

MALEME SECTOR   (Map 2)

18. The essence of the problem in this sector was the defence of the aerodrome and of the long stretch of beach, at any point of which a sea or airborne landing might be effected. Brigadier PUTTICK therefore disposed his forces so as to cover to the best of his ability the whole length of beach. The 5th New Zealand Brigade were located in the area MALEME and were responsible for the protection of the aerodrome and beaches. The 4th New Zealand Brigade were in the area west of GALATOS. It was hoped to make this Brigade mobile and to keep it in

hand as a force reserve.

19. Since the brunt of the fighting fell upon the 5th Infantry Brigade, an outline of the instructions issued by their Commander will be of interest.

20. The Brigade was ordered to maintain a defensive position running east and west from PLATANIAS to the TAVRONITIS river with special regard to the defence of MALEME aerodrome. In the event of the enemy making an airborne or seaborne attack on any part of the area the Brigade was to counterattack immediately.

21. The role of the 28th (Maori) Battalion was to prevent an enemy advance towards CANEA or on the heights south of PLATANIAS, and to be available for counterattack.

22. The role of the New Zealand Engineers was to patrol the beach and road and to hold their position by fire.

23. In the event of an enemy attack from west of the TAVRONITIS river, the 21st Battalion was to move and hold the line of the river facing west on the left of the 22nd Battalion. In the event of the 23rd Battalion being ordered forward, it was to be prepared to occupy that unit's position and to launch a further counterattack on the beach or aerodrome.

24. The 22nd Battalion was primarily to defend the aerodrome. The Battalion was instructed to cover the whole area of the aerodrome and the approaches to it by fire. The fire of mortars was to be held until an actual landing had taken place on the beach or aerodrome. In the event of a landing being made on the aerodrome, support and reserve companies were to be utilised for immediate counterattack under cover of mortar and machine gun fire. 'I' tanks would assist.

25. Three platoons of machine guns were available to support the Brigade.

26. Artillery were to bring fire to bear on the aerodrome and beaches. Bren carriers were to search areas in the immediate vicinity of the brigade and to counterattack.

27. Controlled fire was to be directed against low flying aircraft only after it had become obvious that landings by parachutists or airborne troops were to be made. The greatest volume of fire was then to be delivered.

28. While the above preparations were being put in hand it became increasingly evident that the scale of air attack that the enemy was preparing would exceed anything that had hitherto been experienced. The enemy's first efforts were concentrated on shipping in SUDA BAY harbour, and many who had seen the PIRAEUS become a graveyard for British shipping were to witness a similar scene at SUDA BAY. Indeed, before the attack materialised the possibility of being able to continue to supply the garrison already caused anxiety. Many ships were sunk bringing vital stores. Those that reached harbour in safety were unlikely to survive the period required for unloading.

29. While attacks against shipping continued, enemy air action

was also directed against anti-aircraft gun positions and communications. Eventually, from the 14th onwards, systematic attacks were directed against our aerodromes and it was soon clear that it would be impossible to operate any of our own aircraft. After many had been destroyed on the ground it was decided to withdraw those that remained.

30. Meanwhile, reinforcements were sent from Middle East in an endeavour to meet the impending threat. The 2nd Leicesters disembarked at HERAKLION and the Argyll and Sutherland Highlanders were also warned to sail. A number of guns, together with a few 'I' tanks and light tanks, were also sent.

31. The supply situation was becoming increasingly difficult. Important stores had to be rushed across in destroyers and this could only be done during moonless periods. In order to be well clear of the island by daylight, they had to sail by 03.00 hours. In view of these difficulties hurried reconnaissances were made of the southern beaches with a view to studying the possibility of getting stores across from that side of the island.

NAVAL ASPECT

32. In face of incessant enemy air activity the question of supply via southern beaches was carefully considered. There was no lack of beaches to suit any weather conditions but road access to and from all except SELINOS KASTELLI and TYMBAKI was difficult and required mule transport for the southern five or six miles.

33. In order to accelerate the discharge of cargoes at SUDA to compete with the "Eleventh Hour Supply Rush", an organization was set up to coordinate the berthing and unloading of ships and transport to clear the dock area. (The first rule of the port was that discharged cargo must not be left on the pier or in the dock area.) This organization, known as the Port Control Staff, produced results, but some time elapsed before these results reached the level which was vital to the maintenance of our forces on the island. The composition of this Port Control Staff was as follows:

> King's Harbour Master (Chairman)
> Sea Transport Officer
> Naval officer in charge of caiques and local craft
> Greek Naval Liaison officer
> Army representatives for Dock Labour
> > Transportation
> > Movement Control
> and all other necessary Army Services
> Royal Air Force representative.

34. The Port Control Staff met daily at 17.00 hours to plan the next day's work and once this was established and understood by all authorities the work progressed with greatly increased efficiency.

35. It was definitely established that in the dock area there must be a Senior Military officer with a competent staff to administer the whole of the personnel employed. He is responsible for the routine, accommodation, discipline and feeding of the dock labour. He provides guards, sentries, military police and patrols. He requires

a security staff and the whole dock area and accommodation area for the dock personnel must be kept under most careful supervision. The provision of canteen facilities, tea, latrines, cover, fire parties and first aid posts are most important and it is essential that the system of air raid warnings is suitable to the scale and type of attack. A.P.A.D. scheme and provision of fire-fighting appliances must be decided upon in cooperation with the local Naval authorities.

AIR ASPECT

36. From the 1st to the 12th of May the enemy made constant attacks upon our shipping going to and from CRETE and while at SUDA BAY. Protection at sea was provided mainly by Blenheims of No. 30 Squadron, some of which continued operating in CRETE until the 15th of May. The actual withdrawal of the Squadron to EGYPT began on 7th May as aircraft became unfit for operations and convoy duty diminished.

37. During the same period a number of attacks were made on our aerodromes in CRETE, the scale of these attacks showing a steady increase after 13th May. These attacks and the operations in the first half of the month imposed such a heavy strain on our small fighter force that by the 19th May only seven fighter aircraft were fit for operations. In fact it had become clear that if our remaining fighters were not removed from the island they would either be destroyed on the ground or shot down by sheer weight of numbers. No large scale fighter reinforcements were available in EGYPT. It was therefore decided by the S.A.F.O. CRETE in consultation with the G.O.C., to fly the remaining serviceable aircraft back to EGYPT on the 19th May until the scale of enemy attack lessened or reinforcements became available. During the period they were operating in CRETE these fighters had destroyed at least 23, and probably 31 enemy aircraft.

38. Early in May it had become known that the enemy was collecting large airborne forces for an attack on CRETE, and an endeavour was made to interfere with his air concentrations in GREECE. From the 13th to the 19th of May Greek aerodromes were attacked nightly by Wellington aircraft operating from EGYPT, and on the morning of 17th May Beaufighters made an attack on German aircraft at MOLAOI, ARGOS and HASSANI aerodromes. MARITZA and GALATO in RHODES were also attacked by Wellingtons.

39. The full extent of the damage caused by these attacks is not known, but a number of enemy aircraft were definitely destroyed. The operations were particularly difficult owing to the mountainous nature of the country round the Greek aerodromes and the absence of any moon. Moreover lack of sufficient long range aircraft made it impossible ever to develop these attacks on a scale likely to cause any major alteration of the enemy plan.

PART III   THE ATTACK AND EVACUATION

(20th May to 31st May, 1941)

THE FIGHTING ON MAY 20th.   (Maps 2, 2a, 3, 4.)

MALEME Sector (Maps 2, and 3.)

1.   Soon after dawn on May 20th, the fringe of the aerodrome at MALEME and the greater part of the area occupied by the 22nd Battalion was subjected to a heavy air attack. At 07.45 hours this became intense and continued for more than an hour. In the words of the Officer Commanding the 22nd Battalion, who had won the V.C. in the last war, "The Somme, Messines and Passchendael were mere picnics compared to the bombardment on this morning." Visibility was obliterated by the clouds of dust and smoke that resulted and under cover of the effective screen a number of gliders, estimated at between 50 and 100, landed in the river bed to the west of the aerodrome. This achieved a measure of surprise, for it was generally expected that the bombardment would lift and that parachutists would then descend. Many heads were therefore still down when the gliders landed and literally swamped the defenders in the area of the river bed.

2.   Independent witnesses from the 22nd Battalion express the opinion that the area chosen for glider landings was bombed until the last moment when the barrage shifted for sufficient distance to make a clearing for the gliders, at the same time giving the impression that the whole area was still being bombed. Heads were thus effectively kept down.

3.   The result was that by the time the parachutists descended, glider borne troops were already organized and able to give them covering fire. It should be noted that whereas the glider borne troops arrived complete, parachutists required time to collect their arms and equipment, which arrived in separate parachutes.

4.   The success of the glider attack enabled the enemy to build up a firm base in the river bed, from which their initial soon debouched.

5.   Meanwhile wave after wave of troop carriers flew over the area disgorging their contents with clocklike precision. It was an uncanny sight. Soon the sky was thick with great umbrellas floating earthward. The main areas selected for descent were the river bed to the west of the aerodrome, east of MALEME village, in the valley between GALATOS and the prison, and near the hospital. Some troop carriers also crash landed on the beach.

6.   In all cases where parachutists landed in the vicinity of troops they were immediately dealt with. Indeed, the defenders have little to fear in such cases, but the few who survived caused confusion. Even the odd sniper made intercommunication difficult, for when the telephone lines had been cut, orders could only be sent by runner and in some cases it became necessary to use officers in carriers. The enemy was quick to exploit his footing in the river bed and throughout the day exerted heavy pressure against the western portion of the sector held by the 22nd Battalion. The difficulties of the Battalion were increased by the infiltration

southwards of troops who had crash landed on the beach near MALEME village. In spite of gallant counter attacks assisted by 'I' tanks the situation became grave and at nightfall the Commanding Officer considered his Battalion in danger of being cut off. He therefore decided to withdraw to the general line occupied by 23 and 21 Battalions.

7. It was unfortunate that the 'I' tanks employed in these counter attacks broke down, for it had been intended that they should be kept in hand and concealed until troop carriers attempted to land.

8. In the area occupied by the 4th New Zealand Brigade the situation was in hand at nightfall. The enemy had been ejected from No. 7 General Hospital and from GALATOS, both of which he had captured during the day. He was, however, in considerable strength in the area of the prison and to the west of it.

SUDA BAY Sector. (Map 3)

9. South and southwest of CANEA, landings by parachutists followed by gliders took place at the same time as the attack on MALEME. The main objective of the gliders appears to have been the heavy anti-aircraft batteries in that area. Partly owing to surprise and partly owing to the fact that very few gunners had rifles, the enemy wiped out at least one gun crew.

10. A company of the Rangers and the Royal Perivolians were thrown into some confusion by this attack. The latter were ably rallied by Captain PAGE, their commander, and by noon the enemy had been mopped up. Bren carriers were used to assist. The enemy remained in strength in the prison area.

11. Many parachutists landed within a few hundred yards of the house occupied by His Majesty the King of Greece. Escorted by Colonel BLUNT, the Military Attache, and a small party of New Zealanders, the King made a perilous escape over the mountains, partly on foot and partly by mule. He reached the south coast safely and was rescued by a British destroyer.

12. After depositing their loads, many into the jaws of death, the grim procession of troop carriers moved slowly out to sea. They flew very low and had chosen a corridor where they would be immune from our located anti-aircraft gun positions. Concealed or mobile guns might have wrought havoc. They used the same corridor on the following day.

13. On the AKROTIRE Peninsular about eleven gliders landed soon after dawn. Again, their objective appears to have been the anti-aircraft gun positions in the area. In one case they landed on an abandoned position. Survivors were unfortunately able to make use of the gun pit as cover. The Northumberland Hussars and a company of the Rangers, who were defending the peninsular, took heavy toll of the gliders and only a few scattered survivors remained. Snipers, however became tiresome during the day, particularly in the neighbourhood of Force Headquarters. Most of the glider troops were killed before they had emerged. It was found that the ammunition was stored in the forepart of the glider and that if fire was directed against this there was a good chance of the glider blowing up. In one case a grenade was used with good effect against the enemy after they had got out of the glider and were standing around it.

HERAKLION Sector. (Map 4)

14.   Meanwhile the defences at HERAKLION had been subjected to a heavy bombardment from 16.00 hours to 17.00 hours and it is estimated that about four battalions of parachutists were then dropped on the areas west and south of the town, north and south of the road leading along the aerodrome, and in the valley east of the aerodrome. In accordance with the Brigade Commander's plan, immediate counterattacks were launched by all, including Sector Headquarters, tanks, and Greeks. All areas inside the British perimeter were clear of the enemy by 21.30 hours and extremely heavy casualties had been inflicted on the enemy. Fighting continued in the town and on the outskirts throughout the night.

RETIMO Sector. (Map 4a)

15.   A similar attack was delivered against RETIMO about the same hour. Although the aerodrome remained intact and the bulk of the parachutists were destroyed, parties of the enemy remained in strength to the southeast and a party about 100 strong were able to install themselves in the neighbourhood of a church between RETIMO and the aerodrome. This party severed road communication both between Force Headquarters and the forces protecting RETIMO aerodrome, and between Force Headquarters and HERAKLION. The Greeks fought hard and were warmly praised by Brigadier VASEY.

16.   It is estimated that on the first day of the fighting the number of enemy troops which landed from the air was as follows:-

CANEA	1,800
MALEME	1,700
RETIMO	1,700
HERAKLION	2,000

Few invaders can have received a hotter reception than German parachutists received on this day and survivors will not lightly embark again on such exploits.

The Royal Navy and the Royal Air Force take part in the land fighting.

17.   No account of the fighting on this day would be complete without reference to the gallant fight put up by many sailors and airmen who unwittingly and suddenly found themselves acting as infantrymen. One Naval officer in his report gives a vivid account of his impressions:-

"We were a motley collection about 200 strong. We didn't know where our own people were; we didn't know where the enemy were; many people had no rifles. Many people had rifles and no ammunition. Everyone was desperately tired, thirsty and hungry. We had no food and no water; we had no objective to make for. If anyone fired at you, he might be

(a) an enemy,
(b) a friend who thought you were an enemy,
(c) a friend or an enemy who didn't know what the hell you were,
(d) someone not firing at you at all."

Indeed, obscurity seems to be characteristic of most land battles.

THE GERMAN PLAN

18. It may be well at this juncture to pause and consider the German plan for the capture of CRETE, the outline of which is clear from captured documents. The task was to be carried out by the XIth Flying Corps which was to be divided into three groups:-

>   Eastern Group - Objective HERAKLION
>   Central Group - Objectives RETIMO, CANEA and SUDA.
>   Western Group - Objective MALEME

The Western Group had orders to establish contact with the Central Group.

19. Detailed orders for the taking of CANEA were captured and it may be of interest to consider these in some detail.

20. The forces detailed for this task were to comprise:-

>   7 Air Division (less one parachute regiment and 2 Bn., 2 parachute Regiment).
>   100 Mountain Regiment.
>   Two companies Storm Regiment.
>   Parachute Pioneer Battalion.
>   Parachute A.A. and M.G. Battalion.
>   Parachute Medical Battalion.

21. One parachute regiment was to be in the second wave which was due to capture RETIMO eight hours after the time fixed for the capture of CANEA. Fighting units of this Regiment, as soon as the situation permitted, were to capture British M.T. with a view to enabling them to move to CANEA.

22. Part of the division was to be landed by sea near MALEME.

23. Two companies were detailed to clear the area west of CANEA as far as GALATOS, south of CANEA as far as the mountains and eastwards as far as the western point of SUDA BAY. This detachment was then to capture CANEA and to put the military and civil authorities out of action.

24. Previous to the landings either by glider or parachutes, strong enemy fighter aircraft formations were to attack identified British objectives and in particular the anti-aircraft batteries round SUDA BAY and south of CANEA, the barracks in CANEA and identified encampments west of CANEA and southeast of ALIKIANU. GALATOS was to be kept under observation.

25. One company Storm Regiment was to land at Zero on the high ground in the southwestern part of the AKROTIRE Peninsular east of CANEA; another company of the Storm Regiment was to land in the area between the southern outskirts of CANEA and northeast of PERIVOLIA.

26. At Zero plus 15 one battalion and one company parachute A.A. and M.G. battalion was to land between the road ALIKIANU-CANEA and the road CANEA-GALATOS just east and northeast of GALATOS.

27. It should be noted in passing that the gliders appeared to carry the Storm Troops which landed fifteen minutes before the parachutists. A similar timetable was reported by our troops at MALEME and it was this fact as has been pointed out above, which

contributed largely to the surprise achieved by the Germans.

28.   The Storm Company landing at AKROTIRI was to destroy anti-aircraft batteries on the high ground to the southwest of the peninsular as well as other positions, occupy the Royal Villa and hold the high ground (it is thought that the Germans were under the impression that Flagstaff House, where General FREYBURG was installed, was occupied by the King of Greece.) Subsequently this company was to prevent enemy attacks from CANEA towards the southeast and from SUDA towards the west as well as any enemy disembarkation in SUDA BAY.

29.   The Storm company landing south of CANEA was given the task of destroying anti-aircraft batteries, the wireless station south of CANEA and the supply dump southeast of CANEA. Subsequently it was to push forward towards the company on the peninsular.

30.   The parachutists were to make an attack on the enemy encampments west of CANEA and block the roads CANEA-ALIKIANU and CANEA-GALATOS with a view to preventing the British attacking from CANEA. The coastal road was also to be blocked. Reconnaissances were to be carried out up to AY MARINA. When the situation in their area had been cleared up the battalion was to occupy the southwest boundary of CANEA and prevent any enemy advance from CANEA to the southwest or west. If the situation permitted the battalion was to advance into CANEA and secure the centre of the town and the port.

31.   One battalion was to destroy the supply dump on the ALIKIANU-CANEA road. As the situation cleared, the battalion was to post a covering party to its rear and move forward between the mountains and PERIVOLIA eastwards with its centre of gravity to the right. Eventually it was to reconnoitre as far as SUDA BAY and prevent the advance of enemy forces from SUDA to the west. The road SUDA-CANEA was to be blocked.

32.   The reserve was to be located in the olive groves immediately southeast of the supply dump on the ALIKIANU-CANEA road and to be prepared to attack in the general direction of PERIVOLIA on CANEA as well as in the direction of SUDA BAY.

CONTINUATION OF THE FIGHTING IN THE MALEME AND SUDA BAY AREAS

33.   Throughout the next two days the enemy continued to land reinforcements from the air, and independent witnesses state that on one day alone no less than 600 German troop carriers landed on MALEME aerodrome. Tribute must be paid to our opponent who continued to land on the aerodrome although it was constantly under the fire of our artillery. From a distance they appeared to be sailing into certain death. They paid a heavy price.

34.   On the 21st it was still hoped to recapture the aerodrome and restore the situation. Enemy air action made movement virtually impossible by day and it was therefore decided that a counter attack should be made by night. Orders were issued for the 20th Battalion to be brought up and the general plan was for the attack to be made astride the road with the 20th Battalion on the right of the road and the 28th (Maori) Battalion on the left. Battalions formed up west of PLATANEAS and were ordered to pause about four miles to the

west before delivering the final assault. The attack was made in the face of great difficulties and great credit is due to the 20th Battalion which had to evict Germans from the maze of houses along the coast into which they had infiltrated before the Battalion reached its final jumping-off place. The enemy showed little inclination to fight and ran, leaving machine guns and mortars in our hands. But daylight had now broken and the enemy air force intervened to save the defenders. Even if they had possessed the tools, consolidation by the attackers in daylight would have been impossible in the face of this new found defensive barrage, deadly in its accuracy. The battalions were therefore forced to withdraw after so nearly accomplishing their mission. Indeed, under conditions where the enemy is completely superior in the air, it would seem that the only real chance of success for ground troops is to operate by night and to complete operations in sufficient time to allow of digging in before daylight.

35. Throughout the 22nd troop carriers continued to land. Our guns were still shelling the aerodrome, but they had suffered many casualties. Under normal circumstances they would not have been in action. It was only owing to the fact that number of gunners evacuated from GREECE were serving as infantry that casualties could be continually replaced. On the same day the enemy attacked against GALATOS and drove in the defences, but the situation was eventually cleared.

36. During the nights 21st/22nd and 22nd/23rd, the Royal Navy intercepted and sank many enemy small craft transporting troops and on the second night bombarded MALEME aerodrome. The knowledge that the Fleet was operating close at hand had a most heartening effect on our troops. The price that was being paid was not realized.

37. Meanwhile enemy troops who had landed near the prison began to infiltrate northwards towards AY MARINA. The fact that the 20th Battalion had been sent forward to counterattack left a dangerous gap on the coast and there was a risk that communications with the 5th Brigade might be cut and that the situation of that Brigade might become difficult. On the 23rd, therefore, with a view to closing this gap, the 5th Brigade was ordered to withdraw west of AY MARINA to a position formerly occupied by the 28th (Maori) Battalion. The withdrawal was carried out in daylight with little interference from the air, but the Germans attacked heavily in the afternoon and the situation became critical. The line was now held by the 4th Brigade, but throughout the next two days the Germans continued to exert pressure against them and they were forced to withdraw on the night of 25th/26th leaving the 5th Brigade again to hold the line which was now withdrawn just west of the hospital.

38. It should be mentioned here that the movements of the New Zealand Division at this juncture were being carried out under conditions of extreme difficulty. Apart from the heavy pressure of the enemy both from the air and on the ground, there were few means of intercommunication except by runner. Furthermore, in the absence of tools, positions had to be chosen where the minimum amount of digging would be required.

GENERAL FREYBURG MOVES HIS HEADQUARTERS

39. On the 24th and 25th, CANEA was heavily bombed and virtually destroyed. It was therefore considered advisable for Force

Headquarters to move to a position a few miles east of SUDA on the coastal road. The previous Headquarters on the heights to the east of CANEA had the advantage of a commanding view over the whole battlefield, but this advantage was outweighed by the depressing view that unfolded itself. The continuous stream of troop carriers pouring into MALEME was clearly visible. Furthermore the whole sky to the west was clouded with enemy aircraft continually diving, bombing and machine gunning our troops. In the immediate foreground CANEA was at intervals subjected to the heaviest bombing, the blast of which shook Headquarters. Over the hills to the east and southeast lay a pall of black smoke from burning ships in SUDA BAY. It was a distracting and unhealthy atmosphere for General FREYBURG and his staff.

40. Signals unfortunately received short notice of the move and communications were handicapped on the critical day which followed.

MAJOR GENERAL WESTON APPOINTED TO COMMAND ALL FORCES IN AREA SUDA-CANEA

41. It will be appreciated that the withdrawal of the New Zealand Division was about to cause a most confused situation round CANEA. The Division was withdrawing on to the CANEA garrison, which was under the command of Major General WESTON. Command of this garrison, composed mainly of improvised units of all natures was already proving to be no mean task. In face of this situation it was considered essential to have only one commander in the area and on the morning of the 26th, General FREYBURG appointed General WESTON to command, placing Brigadier PUTTICK under his orders.

42. General WESTON's forces were at this time disposed on a north and south line through MOURNIES. A mixed brigade had been formed under Lieutenant Colonel HELY, 106 R.H.A., and held the line as under:-

```
Right    - Royal Perivolians (Captain PAGE)
Centre   - "S" Battery, Royal Marines
Left     - 2/2 Australian Field Regiment
Reserve  - 106 R.H.A. (250 rifles) and
           2 Greek Battalion
```

The Rangers were in reserve on St. John's Hill and were subsequently withdrawn, together with the Northumberland Hussars, to form a Force Reserve with the 1st Welch.

43. Meanwhile the improvised 19th Australian Brigade under Brigadier VASEY, who had been placed under the New Zealand Division, was holding a creek a mile west of MOURNIES. This added still further to the confusion of the situation.

THE CRITICAL 26th of MAY

44. General FREYBURG informed General WESTON in the morning of the 26th that he proposed sending up the Welch Regiment, the Rangers and the Northumberland Hussars to relieve the New Zealand Division. It was General FREYBURG's intention to hold the position at all costs and in particular with a view to covering the arrival of a destroyer which was due that night with the bulk of LAYFORCE and certain essential stores.

45. General WESTON visited Brigadier PUTTICK about 18.00 hours and informed him of the proposed relief. Meanwhile enemy pressure

continued and Brigadier PUTTICK stated emphatically that his troops would be unable to hold out another day. General WESTON stated that the decision was of such importance that he must refer to the General Officer Commanding in Chief.

46. In the late afternoon the situation deteriorated rapidly. The enemy had penetrated on to some high ground to the north and, the 2nd Greek Battalion to the south having been overwhelmed, he was also making progress around that flank. In the absence of orders from General WESTON, and although no relief had yet arrived, Brigadier PUTTICK, in consultation with Brigadier VASEY, appreciated that the risk of encirclement was real and decided to withdraw at once to a new line along 42nd Street, immediately west of SUDA.

47. The above decision was reached about 22.00 hours. Meanwhile General FREYBURG had issued an order that the line was to be held, but the order was only received when the withdrawal had started.

48. It was unfortunate that the Rangers, the Welch Regiment and the Northumberland Hussars did not move till midnight. They had received orders to be ready to move by 20.30 hours. If they had moved at that hour they would have realized that the New Zealand withdrawal had become inevitable. In the event, they went forward expecting to find New Zealanders in front and the Royal Perivolians on their left.

49. Before dawn the Welch Regiment was in position in the old line about one mile west of the bridge on the western outskirts of CANEA. They sent out patrols both to the west and to the south with a view to getting contact with the New Zealanders and the Perivolians. None of these patrols returned and it became evident soon after daylight that they were in a difficult position. The enemy appeared to have broken through the centre of the Welch Regiment and to be steadily working round the southern flank. Several attempts were made to get messages back to Force Headquarters but none got through. In view of the ever-increasing threat the Commanding Officer decided soon after midday that he must withdraw and he therefore issued instructions for both battalions to move back and reorganize west of SUDA. The battalions had already suffered very heavy casualties in the fighting while holding the line forward and they were faced with still greater difficulties in their efforts to withdraw. The Germans had already nearly encircled them by a wide movement round their southern flank. Furthermore, since there were no troops in the neck of the peninsular, the German troops in that area were free to move forward with mortars and effectively to impede the withdrawal.

50. Before participating in the above fighting, the Welch Regiment and the Northumberland Hussars had been fully employed mopping up the AKROTIRI peninsular, where in addition to the gliders which had landed on the first day a caique had also succeeded in reaching the shore. A large scale sweep was carried out by two companies of the Welch Regiment and many of the enemy were rounded up. But the small forces available made it impossible completely to clear the area. It is unfortunate that the confusion described above resulted in such heavy casualties. Their efforts, however, may have done much to stem the tide. General WESTON had made every effort to send orders to these units to withdraw.

THE WITHDRAWAL FROM THE SUDA-CANEA AREA TO SPHAKIA

The decision to withdraw

51. By the morning of the 27th, General FREYBURG realized that evacuation had become inevitable. He therefore reported the situation to Middle East, and although no decision was received until the evening, his hand had been already forced. He ordered General WESTON to organize the rearguard while his own Headquarters moved to SPHAKIA with a view to organizing the evacuation.

Difficulties of Command

52. The difficulties which confronted General WESTON were great. Many of the few despatch riders with which he started had their motor bicycles stolen by retreating troops. Liaison officers, even if they existed, lacked transport. As a result, General WESTON found himself unable to exercise control during the first two days of the withdrawal. During this period it became a Brigadiers' battle. Close collaboration between Brigadiers HARGEST, commanding the 5th New Zealand Brigade, VASEY, commanding the 19th Australian Brigade, and Colonel LAYCOCK, commanding LAYFORCE alone enabled the initial part of the withdrawal to be conducted in security.

Withdrawal to the "Saucer"

53. The 4th New Zealand Brigade had been withdrawn on the night of the 26th/27th to STYLOS and later ordered to move back to the ASKIPHIO PLAIN, known as the "Saucer", with a view to preventing a possible enemy parachute descent in that area. A detachment of this Brigade was also sent to the area VRYSES to prevent any enemy threat from GEORGOPOULIS.

54. The early rearguard fighting was therefore left to LAYFORCE, 5th New Zealand Brigade, and the 19th Australian Brigade. The 5th and 19th Brigades were working together as one force. Colonel LAYCOCK had been ordered to find the rearguard on the 27th, and continued to do so until ordered by General WESTON to withdraw on the 29th. During the same period, however, the 5th and 19th Brigades made their own protective dispositions. In fact there were two independent forces leap-frogging through each other, each finding its own protection.

55. Disembarking on the night of the 26th/27th, LAYFORCE, who had left ALEXANDRIA under the impression that the situation was in hand, were immediately placed under General WESTON and ordered to take up a rearguard position east of SUDA. A part of LAYFORCE which had landed earlier was already assisting on the 42nd Street line.

56. The position east of SUDA was held by LAYFORCE until after dark on the night 27th/28th, when the 5th and 19th Brigades withdrew through them. Leaving a small party near the fork where the STYLOS road breaks off from the coast road, Colonel LAYCOCK, with the bulk of his force, moved back to a position in the area BALALI INN. The detachment left near the coast was unfortunately overwhelmed, the enemy having moved round their southern flank across country. Indeed the enemy appears to have made a serious effort to place himself astride the road STYLOS - SPHAKIA with a view to cutting off the withdrawal. Later he also made contact with the left of Colonel LAYCOCK's new position at BALALI INN but was driven off.

57. By arrangement with Brigadier VASEY, Colonel LAYCOCK had been reinforced on the above position by 2/3 Australian Battalion. Three 'I' tanks had also been placed under this command. These did invaluable work throughout the withdrawal, keeping the enemy at a respectful distance. At one juncture Colonel LAYCOCK himself owed his own escape to an 'I' tank that came to his rescue in an very exposed position.

58. Certain demolitions were to be carried out under Colonel LAYCOCK's orders, but one was blown prematurely without his orders and considerable delay caused to retreating troops who were still on the enemy side of the obstacle.

59. LAYFORCE was eventually withdrawn by General WESTON's orders to IMVROS.

60. Meanwhile the 5th New Zealand and 19th Australian Brigades had withdrawn from the 42nd Street position during the night of 27th/28th. They moved to STYLOS which they reached about 03.30 hours, having left a company of Maoris south of the coastal fork road in the same area as the detachment of LAYFORCE. At 06.30 hours their left was attacked by a strong force of Germans who had made their way across country. Presumably this was the same force which attacked LAYFORCE later in the day in their position further to the south.

61. In face of the above threat, although his brigade had been on the move most of the night, Brigadier HARGEST decided to continue the withdrawal by day at the risk of interference from enemy air action. A long and gruelling march followed. Moving off at 10.00 hours on the 28th, the brigade halted at 15.00 hours for three hours at VRYSES and was on the move again at 18.00 hours. There were still twelve miles to cover up a winding hill to the top of the pass. The endurance and discipline displayed on this march was a credit to all. Fortunately enemy air attacks were not on the scale that might have been expected. The brigade reached SYNKARES about 03.00 hours on the 29th, having left 23 Battalion in position at the top of the pass. The enemy made contact with this battalion but did not press home an attack.

62. By the morning of the 29th therefore, the bulk of the 4th, 5th and 19th Brigades had reached the ASKIPHIO plain or "Saucer".

The withdrawal from the "Saucer" to SPHAKIA and Evacuation.

63. As soon as the bulk of his force was concentrated in the "Saucer", General WESTON was again able to assume control. He assembled commanders of 4, 5, and 19 Brigades at a conference in the afternoon of the 29th when orders were given for all to move to an assembly area on the escarpment that evening. The 4th Brigade were to hold the ASKIPHIO plain that evening until nightfall.

64. The intention was that all should be within reach of the beach in time for evacuation on the following night. Rearguard duty now fell to the 19th Australian Brigade, to the Royal Marines, and to LAYFORCE. The Royal Marines were placed under Brigadier VASEY who was also given two 'I' tanks and three Bren carriers. Brigadier VASEY disposed the bulk of his force on the high ground about VITSILOKOUMOS detaching 2/8 Battalion to watch the ravine west of KOMITADES. LAYFORCE was ordered to watch the ravine to the northeast of KOMITADES.

65. The move started at 18.00 hours. The enemy had made contact with the 4th Brigade about 16.30 hours and brought heavy machine gun fire to bear upon their positions. The Brigade still had retained a few guns and these were used at nightfall. Indeed the enemy showed consistent lack of enterprise in operating by night. Troops reached their allotted assembly area about 22.00 hours.

66. The difficulties of the evacuation were increased by the nature of the country. It will be noted on Map 5 that the road to SPHAKIA ends in a series of hairpin bends which lead abruptly down from a height of about 2,000 feet to the plain below. The lower half of the road being unfinished was covered with rough stones and came to an abrupt end about 400 feet above sea level. The plain below was of the roughest scrub and covered with loose boulders, and was crossed only by a few ill defined tracks. It is to be regretted that many of the more ill-disciplined troops in their anxiety to reach the beaches had jumped lorries and cars, which they had in many cases abandoned in the middle of the hairpin portion of the road. These vehicles, apart from precluding any possibility of hiding our intentions from the enemy, became the object of continuous attacks from enemy aircraft. Soon the road was littered with burning vehicles and became blocked. There being no signal communications, touch between the beach area and the top of the escarpment had to be maintained on foot. The climb required at least two hours to complete and was always hazardous in the face of enemy air attack.

67. The first evacuations had taken place during the nights of the 28th/29th and 29th/30th, when wounded and mostly non-fighting troops were embarked. It will be appreciated that walking wounded alone could be embarked, but determination not to fall into enemy hands impelled many of the more seriously wounded to attempt the difficult journey down to the beach. It would be difficult to describe the hardships these men endured. The movement by night over this rough country demanded superhuman efforts. Scarcity of water, only to be found in a few wells, added to their sufferings.

68. At dawn on May 30th the enemy made contact with the rearguard. The two tanks and three carriers of Brigadier VASEY's force fought a most successful rearguard action. At this juncture, under cover of the retiring tanks, Major PARKER of the 42nd Field Company personally supervised the blowing up of many demolitions. A party of Royal Marines also, who had taken up a position well in advance of the main rearguard position, effectively delayed the enemy with their bren guns. The Germans only felt their way cautiously forward and although making contact later with Brigadier VASEY's force they were easily driven off. A small party of the enemy, however, broke through along the ravine to the west of KOMITADES. They were attacked and driven off by 4 New Zealand Brigade.

69. All troops now had to be embarked on the nights 30th/31st and 31st/1st which was the last. The 5th New Zealand Brigade and such of Brigadier VASEY's force as could reach the beaches in time were the last to embark. Major General WESTON also himself stayed until the last night, General FREYBURG having been ordered to go back to Middle East the previous night.

70. The main difficulty now was to collect troops from their scattered hiding places in the assembly area, move them to the beach, and arrange priority of embarkation. Many administrative troops had

embarked on the first two nights. General FREYBURG therefore decided that during the last two nights fighting troops should have priority. In the event many skilled personnel, particularly of the Royal Army Ordnance Corps were left behind.

71.   The difficulties during the last days were increased by the shortage of rations and water problems. The Royal Navy landed rations on the beach, but the task of man-handling them to the troops in the assembly area up the escarpment and to the rearguard proved almost insuperable. Many rations fell into wrong hands as the neighbourhood of the beaches was filled with ill-disciplined individuals who had made their own way down without orders. A few wells existed but the difficulty again was distribution, partly owing to lack of containers. The importance of early and adequate measures being taken for strong beach control cannot be exaggerated. A strong cordon was eventually established.

72.   As there would be no room for all troops remaining to embark, Major General WESTON detailed Lieutenant Colonel COLVIN of LAYFORCE to remain in charge of those who were to be left on the island. In view of the state of the men and the difficult ration situation, General WESTON considered that no useful purpose could be served by continued resistance. He therefore gave Lieutenant Colonel COLVIN written orders instructing him to collect all senior officers and come to terms with the enemy.

73.   Many perforce had to be left behind. It was unfortunate that the 2/7 Australian Battalion did not reach the beach in time. Brigadier VASEY had already continually split up his Brigade to meet varying situations and the loss of this battalion came as a final bitter blow. The bulk of LAYFORCE were also left behind through a misunderstanding. But the difficulties were great and there was no means of intercommunication between the beaches and the assembly area except by runner. Good signal communication between the beaches and assembly area is all important.

74.   Those who were able to leave the island were indeed fortunate, for the enemy were given a heaven sent opportunity of closing the back door. The dropping of only a few parachutists either in the area of the "Saucer" or the beaches might well have sealed the fate of the retreating and exhausted garrison who, with an enemy on their heels, were in no state to fight on equal terms. Furthermore, the comparatively feeble efforts of the enemy air force to interfere with our withdrawal were in marked contrast to the magnificent co-operation which had been displayed during the earlier fighting.

EVENTS AT HERAKLION AND RETIMO

75.   While the events described above were taking place a gallant defence was being conducted both at HERAKLION and at RETIMO.

HERAKLION

76.   Although the cipher was destroyed at HERAKLION during the first day's fighting, intercommunication was facilitated by the existence of the submarine cable between SUDA and HERAKLION. This only became unserviceable on the 25th, after which, except in clear, it was only possible to communicate through Middle East by the cable between EGYPT and HERAKLION.

77.   Brigadier CHAPPEE's dispositions for the defence of the aerodrome had proved remarkably effective, and the days succeeding the attack were mostly occupied with mopping up operations. In these the light tanks were particularly effective. During the early period, when parachutes were descending, they found their main difficulty was to traverse the turret with sufficient speed. Many eventually stood up in the open and used revolvers. Tommy guns would have proved invaluable. Many of the enemy were run over. As in other sectors, the 'I' tanks broke down.

78.   But meanwhile the enemy was continually being reinforced. Our troops, as at MALEME, could see the continual arrival of troop carriers to the east. They were powerless to intervene. Many aircraft appeared to be landing on MALEA beach.

79.   During the first few days of the fighting, the situation in the western portion of HERAKLION was cleared by the gallant efforts of the Greeks, including militia, helped by about 50 British troops. But the enemy had meanwhile strongly entrenched himself to the west of the town.

80.   On the 23rd two 'I' tanks reached the garrison, having broken through a part of the enemy who were established south of HERAKLION near the TYMBAKI road. These tanks also brought news of the approach of the Argyll and Sutherland Highlanders from the MESSARA PLAIN. On the same day an ultimatum was received from the enemy calling for HERAKLION to surrender and threatening heavy bombing in the event of refusal. The Greek commander agreed to fight on and orders were issued for the complete evacuation of the civilians.

81.   On the following day the town was heavily bombed and more parachutists were landed in the west. With the help of these reinforcements, on the 25th, the enemy delivered an attack on the town from the west but was repulsed by a successful counterattack staged by the Yorkshire and Lancashire Regiment. The enemy suffered heavy casualties in this engagement.

82.   During the night of 25th/26th the Argyll and Sutherland Highlanders who had succeeded in reaching the perimeter, relieved the Leicestershire Regiment who were withdrawn into reserve for mobile operations.

83.   On the same night the German forces west of HERAKLION moved across south of the British perimeter with a view to joining up with the remainder of their force in the area AY LYAS. At dawn the Germans were still moving across and an attack was delivered by the Leicestershire Regiment. Initially successful, the attack was finally held up by an Australian patrol of the 2/11th, which had been cut off, fought its way back, killing 20 Germans at the cost of three casualties to itself.

84.   Vigorous and successful patrolling was carried out on the 27th. On the 28th further reinforcements were seen to land to the east. It was now clear that it was only a matter of time before a major attack was delivered from that area.

85.   Orders for evacuation were received during the early hours of the 28th. Very careful arrangements were made for the firing of weapons and Verey lights by the rear parties until the last possible moment and embarkation was carried out with little interference on the part of the enemy.

RETIMO

86.   Unfortunately the complete story of events at RETIMO is missing since there are few survivors to tell the tale. When no threat materialized against GEORGOPOULIS, Brigadier VASEY and the two battalions there were ordered to the area CANEA. Lieutenant Colonel CAMPBELL then assumed command at RETIMO. The aerodrome never fell into enemy hands. Although it is understood that the Greek battalion which had been placed between the two Australian battalions was overwhelmed, the Australians successfully kept the enemy at bay.

87.   Intercommunication between Force Headquarters and the garrison was only possible by W/T and in clear, since they had no cypher. The establishment of the enemy in the area of the church east of RETIMO town had cut all other means of communication. A serious effort was made to dislodge them on the 24th. A company of the Rangers supported by two 2 pounder guns was sent from CANEA with orders to attack from the west. Meanwhile one of the Australian battalions from the aerodrome was ordered to deliver a simultaneous attack from the east. Unfortunately a co-ordinated attack did not materialize. The Rangers failed to make contact with the Australians and the attack failed. The enemy had been established for four days and a day attack with inadequate supporting fire was perhaps a hazardous operation.

88.   Meanwhile the enemy continued to reinforce the area to the southeast of the aerodrome and it was clear that a heavy attack would eventually be launched. The situation of the garrison was also becoming serious owing to the shortage of rations and medical equipment. This, however, was alleviated by the Royal Navy who at great risk and in the face of an obscure situation, sent out an M.L.C. from SUDA with rations and medical stores on the night of the 27th/28th.

89.   Meanwhile the anxieties of General FREYBURG's staff were increased by the problem of communicating the withdrawal order to RETIMO. Obviously it could not be sent in clear. Middle East were therefore asked for the order to be dropped from the air. An aircraft was sent but it is understood that it was not heard of again. The intention was for the garrison to embark at PLAKA BAY.

90.   It is not yet known whether the order was ever received and the full story of RETIMO remains still to be told.

THE NAVAL ASPECT

91.   The Naval problems during this phase may be stated briefly as follows:-

(a) To keep the Commander in Chief MEDITERRANEAN fully informed of the local situation.

(b) To maintain the patrols of the harbour.

(c) To unload damaged ships by night.

(d) To arrange for eleventh hour supply by warship of essential stores and equipment.

(e) To arrange for the re-distribution by water of tanks, food and ammunition.

(f) To inform Commander in Chief MEDITERRANEAN of numbers for evacuation when this had been decided upon.

(g) To evacuate Naval personnel.

(h) To maintain communication with Commander in Chief MEDITERRANEAN.

92.   Before the attack started, alternative arrangements for external communications had been considered. W/T sets manned by Naval personnel were installed at HERAKLION, RETIMO and at Force Headquarters at CANEA. A fourth set was put on board a motor launch for passage to SPHAKIA. Unfortunately this craft was bombed and sunk on the way there.

93.   Arrangements were also made for a portable set at the Naval W/T Station to be placed quickly in a lorry for transport to any place required. Fortunately the Naval W/T Station remained intact until destroyed by us just before the departure of the Naval Staff by road to SPHAKIA, and it was therefore possible to keep the Commander in Chief MEDITERRANEAN informed of the local situation right up to this time. There was then a period of about twelve hours when external communication was not possible as, owing to the bad roads, the portable W/T set in the lorry would not work. When it arrived near SPHAKIA next morning all the valves were found to be broken. Communication was eventually re-established by means of a Royal Air Force set which had previously been sent to SPHAKIA and was maintained until the departure of the Naval Staff.

94.   Normal patrols of the harbour were maintained during the early stages of this phase, but when deliberate attacks on them by day became heavy they were withdrawn by day and ordered to tie up in "hide outs". The maximum possible patrols were maintained throughout by night. Even so the majority of the patrol craft were sunk before the actual evacuation was ordered.

95.   The unloading of damaged ships by night was continued for as long as possible. As these ships could not produce their own steam or lights, another vessel had to be placed alongside for this purpose. One of the patrol craft was used for this and after the early teething troubles had been overcome a reasonable measure of success was achieved. Unloading by day was by this time quite out of the question.

96.   The supply of vital stores, food and ammunition by warship was arranged with the Commander in Chief MEDITERRANEAN. The ships arrived at about midnight and in order to be well clear of the island by daylight they had to leave again by 02.30 hours. Rapid unloading was therefore essential and a careful organization was required to ensure that the pier and jetty were cleared by daylight. Navigational aids were required to assist the ships in coming alongside and parties of men to take their wires were organized.

97. Some days before evacuation had been decided upon the situation appeared to the Naval Staff to be becoming critical. The Naval Officer in charge therefore sent a personal note to the Chief of Staff to the Commander in Chief MEDITERRANEAN giving his appreciation of the situation and outlining a plan for evacuation should it become necessary. This plan had been discussed previously with the D.A. & Q.M.G.

98. When it became obvious that SUDA harbour would shortly be overrun by the enemy, which was before Force Headquarters received orders to evacuate, it was decided to send away all Naval personnel in H.M. ships which were arriving with stores that night, with the exception of a skeleton Naval Staff, W/T staff and Cypher staff. Arrangements were subsequently made for any Naval personnel who missed this passage to have a high priority for evacuation later on. Under these arrangements the great majority of the Naval personnel were evacuated and orders were received for the skeleton staffs who had remained behind to embark on the night of 30th/31st May.

99. During the actual embarkation at SPHAKIA, the maximum number of troops was not always taken off. This was in part due to lack of facilities for intercommunication and partly to the difficult access to the beach, which made it impossible to get people down in a hurry at the last moment.

100. The numbers to be taken off each night were communicated to the Naval officer in charge by the Commander in Chief MEDITERRANEAN. Arrangements were made for that number, plus some spares, to be handy to the beach. These numbers had been decided upon by the Commander in Chief MEDITERRANEAN as he knew his ships would have to fight their way out against heavy air attacks and that an overloaded ship is unmanageable. On every night except the first when wounded only were being embarked and only ships boats were available, the numbers given by the Commander in Chief MEDITERRANEAN were exceeded. This led to a frantic rush of men down the steep approach to the beach which allowed numbers of disorganized troops to be embarked before well disciplined troops who had borne the brunt of the fighting. This caused bitter disappointment and a sense of insecurity amongst the good troops and might well lead to ugly scenes on a beach if disorganized troops get left behindst the last moment.

THE AIR ASPECT

101. With one exception, aircraft which took part in the battle of CRETE were operated from EGYPT.

102. Attacks against enemy aerodromes in GREECE and the DODECANESE were continued after the invasion began, and on the night of the 20th/21st May, TOPOLIA, MENIDI, ELEUSIS and MOLASI were bombed. On the night of the 22nd/23rd May bad weather in the Western Desert made flying impossible and a plan to attack MALEME aerodrome had to be cancelled. These conditions persisted in the Desert for two days. The CANEA area, however, was clear on the night of the 22nd/23rd and three Wellingtons dropped medical stores and rations at RETIMO and HERAKLION. Unfortunately, at RETIMO the supplies fell into the sea.

103.   On the morning of the 23rd of May an attempt was made to send two flights of six Hurricanes each to CRETE from EGYPT. Unfortunately aircraft in the first flight were damaged by a Naval anti-aircraft barrage and only one landed at HERAKLION. Of the remainder two were shot down and three returned to their base. The second flight arrived safely at HERAKLION, but four aircraft had to be returned to EGYPT on 24th May owing to damaged tail wheels. One of the other two was damaged on the ground by enemy action and rendered unserviceable. Thus of the twelve Hurricanes originally despatched to CRETE on the 23rd May, only two were serviceable on the 24th May.

104.   On the afternoon of the 23rd, twelve Blenheims made the first attack on MALEME aerodrome. A second attack was delivered by Blenheims and Marylands later in the afternoon and two long range Hurricanes also machine gunned aircraft on the ground at MALEME. In these attacks a number of enemy aircraft were destroyed and others damaged.

105.   On the night of the 24th MALEME was bombed by eight Wellingtons while, during the day, five long range Hurricanes attacked enemy positions in the HERAKLION area. Medical stores were dropped by Wellingtons at RETIMO on the night of the 24th/25th May.

106.   On the 25th May, Hurricanes and fighter Blenheims despatched to attack MALEME aerodrome at dawn were unable to find the target owing to low cloud and heavy mist. One Hurricane forced landed at HERAKLION. Later in the morning a combined force of Marylands, Blenheims and Hurricanes made a successful attack on MALEME aerodrome. One Hurricane shot down a JU 88 over SUDA BAY and damaged another. In the afternoon MALEME was twice more attacked, and three Blenheims making the second of these raids did not return. The same day reconnaissances for enemy shipping were made in the Aegean Sea.

107.   Four Wellingtons again bombed MALEME on the night of the 25th/26th and a separate attack was made by Wellingtons on SCARPANTO. During the 26th, six Hurricanes attacked MALEME and shot down five JU 52s and damaged others in the air and on the ground. A further attack was made on MALEME at dusk.

108.   During the night of the 26th/27th aircraft on the ground were again bombed. During the 27th May three JU 88s were shot down by a Hurricane fighter patrol. A force of Blenheims despatched at dusk to bomb enemy troop concentrations at CANEA failed to find the objective and bombed the aerodrome at MALEME causing much damage. The same night the same objective was attacked by Wellingtons and another force of four aircraft attacked SCARPANTO.

109.   On the 28th and 29th Hurricanes and Blenheims maintained patrols over H.M. ships en route from EGYPT to CRETE. At night on the 28th a heavy attack was made on SCARPANTO and repeated the following night.

110.   During the night of the 29th/30th MALEME aerodrome was again attacked by Wellingtons and the next night both MALEME and HERAKLION were raided. Fighter protection was again provided for H.M. ships on the 31st May and 1st June. During these patrols at least 18 enemy aircraft were destroyed and many others were either damaged or driven off. On the night of the 31st/1st, HERAKLION and MALEME were again attacked by Wellingtons and supplies were dropped on the beach at SPHAKIA

111.   In paragraph 103 reference was made to the Hurricanes operating from HERAKLION. The pilots of these aircraft were despatched from EGYPT with instructions to attack enemy transport aeroplanes approaching or landing at MALEME. On arrival at HERAKLION, however, these instructions were countermanded by the local military commander and the pilots ordered to act in direct support of our defence forces in that area.

112.   The number of fighter aircraft concerned in this incident was small, and the fact that they were not employed as was intended could in no way have affected the outcome of the operations in CRETE. The principle involved however is of first importance, and the action taken sets a dangerous precedent. In other circumstances, interference with the instructions given to pilots sent on a specific mission without reference to the officer sending them on that mission or to the senior Royal Air Force officer in the actual sphere of operations, might jeopardize the outcome of an entire campaign.

PART IV

SUMMARY OF LESSONS

GENERAL REMARKS

1. It should be emphasised that many of the lessons set out below are solely applicable to conditions where the enemy has the complete air superiority which characterised this campaign.

Ambiguity as to the role of the Garrison

2. From the outset there was ambiguity as to the role of the garrison. Brigadier TIDBURY was given the task of:-

    (a) defending the refuelling base in SUDA BAY, and
    (b) in co-operation with the local Greek forces, preventing and defeating any attempt by a hostile force to gain a foothold in the island.

Whether the task given to Brigadier TIDBURY was practicable with the forces at his disposal is beyond the scope of this Report to say. Four months later, however, when Brigadier GALLOWAY assumed command, the task was modified, and limited solely to the defence of SUDA BAY.

3. Brigadier GALLOWAY's reign was short. Brigadier CHAPPEL, on succeeding him, asked for guidance from Middle East. Major General WESTON, who arrived shortly after, gave as his opinion that the defence of the SUDA BAY and HERAKLION areas should be considered as self-contained and separate problems. Finally, on April 30th, the role of the garrison was defined as being "to deny to the enemy the use of air bases in CRETE". The object was at last clear, but time was moving on.

4. The appointment of five commanders in six months could hardly produce the best results.

5. Broadly, there were two alternatives before General FREYBURG:-

    (a) Partially to disperse his force with a view to protecting both the aerodromes against an airborne and the beaches in their vicinity against a seaborne attack.
    (b) To concentrate his force in four self-contained groups for the immediate defence of the three aerodromes and the base area at SUDA.

General FREYBURG adopted the first course. In order to meet the sea threat considerable dispersion was necessary west of CANEA where the enemy might land at any point on the 12 miles stretch of beach. Dispositions of the New Zealand Division were influenced by that factor. The Commander of the 5th New Zealand Brigade was very anxious about the area west of MALEME aerodrome and it was unfortunate that his intention to place a Greek battalion there had not been put into effect before the attack came.

6. It is interesting to speculate as to whether the adoption of the second solution might have been more profitable. MALEME aerodrome might have remained intact and the rapid reinforcement by airborne troops greatly delayed. It is even possible that the enemy might have been discouraged from continuing his attempts. But the aerodrome at HERAKLION remained intact and yet the enemy were able to land troop carriers to the east and out of reach. The garrisons would in any case have been pinned

under the combined efforts of the encircling parachutists and the permanent air threat overhead. Other landing grounds would soon have been prepared by the parachutists. They had started to prepare one in the valley behind the prison. Furthermore, the Navy was powerless to stop an eventual landing by sea. Indeed, according to the German accounts, the Italians landed in the east of the island, on the 28th; nor had General FREYBURG the resources with which to form a mobile reserve to meet such a threat. The vast length of the coast line and the number of possible landing beaches should constantly be borne in mind. Moreover the means for reconnaissance seaward were lacking and the garrison was virtually blind. It is noteworthy that as a result of the disposition adopted, nearly all the parachutists that landed could not fail to descend near some of the defending troops.

7. Further speculation as to the courses open to General FREYBURG either at this juncture or later when the decision was made to withdraw would be unprofitable. Perhaps the major lesson of this campaign was that to defend with a relatively small force an island as large as CRETE, lying under the permanent domination of enemy fighter aircraft and out of range of our own was impossible.

Failure to prepare defences.

8. With notable exceptions, six months of comparative peace were marked by inertia for which ambiguity as to the role of the garrison was in large measure responsible. If the ultimate result of the fighting could not have been altered in the absence of air support, the difficulties of the enemy could at least have been multiplied if full advantage had been taken of this period to convert the island into a fortress. If engineer resources were lacking, the island had a population of 400,000 inhabitants, the majority of whom were determined, as was shown in the event, to defend their homes. A hive of industry should have been created. Although it was realized that the garrison would ultimately be increased to a division, no defence plan was prepared. There was a marked tendency at one time to regard CRETE as a base for offensive operations without any apparent regard to the advisability of being able to operate from a secure base.

9. Field works, including pill boxes, should have been built in all areas where static defence was required. Possible landing beaches should have been obstructed both against amphibian tanks and crash landing aircraft. Similar steps should have been taken in all areas where aircraft might have landed. The task may have been Herculean; but in the face of an industrious opponent Herculean tasks must be faced.

10. One of the few commanders who appears to have realized the importance of digging, and who had even planned an intensive night and day digging programme was discouraged in his efforts. At least a sufficient reserve of tools and defence stores should have been built up in the island. Desperate efforts were made at the last moment to make amends, but it was too late. Much was lost at sea through enemy air action.

11. The Royal Air Force cannot claim to have shown greater foresight or energy than the Army. A secure base is as important to them as to the Army. From the day the island was occupied, the efforts of every available man, including the civilian population, should have been directed to the preparation and camouflaging of satellite landing grounds, the construction of pens with overhead cover and even in the digging of underground hangars let into the hillsides. The effort required may have been stupendous, but the results might have been far-reaching.

The Air Factor

12.   Until the power of the air arm as a weapon of close support on the battlefield is fully appreciated and exploited, the army will continue to labour under a severe handicap and will be prevented from developing its full force either in attack or defence. German methods must be seriously studied and applied.

13.   Aircraft, by their ability to concentrate quickly at a selected point, can provide the heaviest and most effective supporting barrage yet devised. In effect they can provide the equivalent of an artillery and machine gun barrage with the added advantage that the target is under constant observation, so that the fire can be switched immediately at will. There is no escape. Indeed, it was this concentrated inferno that enabled a comparatively small force to blast its way through our defences. It may be argued that the scale of enemy air superiority obtaining in CRETE was abnormal, but the mobility of the air force, assisted by interior lines, should always enable the attacker to concentrate a mass of aircraft at the chosen point and achieve the requisite air superiority locally, even though it be only for a short time.

14.   As an example of the strength of this close support and the detail with which its preparation is worked out, the following may be instanced. One glider company that landed in the CANEA area had a whole flight of Stukas to support it. The task given to the flight was to bomb anti-aircraft and artillery positions and a group of houses which was the company's objective for three minutes. In addition, this company's operation was covered by twelve Me. 109 and six Me. 110 whose task was to neutralize anti-aircraft batteries and enemy ground troops.

15.   If support of the nature described above is to be effective, constant training and standardized method, particularly as regards intercommunication between ground and air, are required. Hasty improvisation to meet the demands of particular operations cannot give the same results.

Enemy air action and the Supply Problem

16.   Even if no attack had developed, the continued supply of the island garrison would have incurred disastrous shipping losses. Small, fast craft capable of discharging their load on the southern beaches and sailing again within the hours of darkness would have reduced losses. That they were not available betrays lack of study in peace time of the problems of combined operations under modern conditions. During the earlier period, the existence of freight carrying aircraft on a large scale might have eased the supply situation. Although, in the face of enemy air superiority, their use would have been precluded by day, the development of night flying facilities, if the aircraft to use them had been available, might have been well repaid. It is regrettable also that after nearly two years of war, sufficient parachute equipment for the dropping of supplies on a large scale was not available.

The Problem of Fighter Aircraft

17.   The inability to provide fighter protection in CRETE deprived the garrison of the most effective means of defence not only against airborne, but also against seaborne attack. If the Royal Navy successfully prevented one seaborne attempt, it could not, in the face of enemy air

superiority, have continued permanently to operate in the Aegean. Many enemy ships would eventually have reached CRETE unmolested. Furthermore, as has been shown, the land forces would have been incapable of protecting the lengthy coast line.

18.   It is considered that CRETE could only have been defended if at least six fighter squadrons could have been kept up to strength. Was this possible? In view of the lamentable lack of preparation during the preparatory period, it was certainly not possible at the last moment. But if, from the outset, the problem had been tackled with vision, something might have been achieved.

Intercommunication

19.   Intercommunication between Force Headquarters and EGYPT worked well throughout, but although handicapped in CRETE through lack of equipment, the British Army is painfully behind the   German Army in the development of signals communications. A copy of the very thorough Signal arrangements made for the invasion of CRETE was captured and will repay study. Some of our W/T sets appear to have been designed solely with a view to transporting them by car. The possibility of ever having to operate off a road does not appear to have struck the designers. Many sets had to be abandoned because they could not be manhandled and it is recommended that in so far as is practicable, all sets be made in sections sufficiently small to be manhandled.

20.   If some of our difficulties can be attributed to unsuitable equipment, much is due to laziness and lack of imagination. Lines laid on telegraph poles down a main road were not likely to survive when enemy air action became serious. The burying of at least some cable might have been attempted during the six months of the preparatory period.

Discipline and Morale

21.   Unfortunately, lax discipline has permeated many units. Such discipline will not stand the acid test of hardship. Scenes were witnessed during the withdrawal which could only be attributed to a low standard of discipline. The instinct of self-preservation overrode all else. Officers failed to exert the control that might have been expected of them. The effect on morale of enemy air superiority has been mentioned above. Up to a point this was inevitable, but the effects would have been reduced by a higher standard of discipline. During the withdrawal, on occasions when enemy aircraft were inactive, any movement on the part of individuals trying to profit by a lull was greeted by panic shouts of "Lie down". Men crouched in ditches and seemed paralysed. At night, any attempt to put on the lights of a car would be greeted by abuse and, in some cases, by bullets.

22.   The need for troops to take cover and to conceal themselves from enemy aircraft must not override the need for alertness. However heavy the air attack, some men must permanently be on the look out. A sergeant in the Black Watch who gave evidence before the Committee testified to the excellent effect on morale of men judiciously putting their heads up and keeping their eyes on enemy aircraft instead of all crouching continually at the bottom of their slits.

23.   Although the above touches upon certain aspects of discipline only, discipline generally needs tightening. Drill still has its place, and should not, as it is by some, be associated solely with bows and arrows.

ARMY LESSONS

DEFENCE AGAINST GLIDER-BORNE ATTACK AND PARACHUTISTS

Enemy Tactics

24.   The tactics employed by the enemy in CRETE were broadly as follows.

(a) Intense bombing of the area chosen for landing.

(b) Bombing continued, but lifts from the actual corridor chosen for landing.

(c) Gliders land under cover of above and overwhelm surprised defenders. If attack is to be followed by landing of troop carriers, main objective of the glider troops will probably be anti-aircraft batteries.

(d) Parachutists land about fifteen minutes later.

(e) Re-organization.

It should be noted that whereas the glider-borne troops arrive complete with arms and equipment, parachutists need time to unharness and collect them as part is carried in a separate parachute. Parachutists are therefore very vulnerable immediately on landing.

General Measures recommended to meet such Attacks

25.   Alertness is the first essential. A proportion of men, even at the height of the bombing, must be on the look out to guard against surprise. A supply of periscopes with all round vision would be invaluable.

26.   The new danger makes all round defence more than ever essential. Furthermore, owing to the danger of detachments being momentarily isolated, the smallest posts should be self-contained as regards ammunition, food and water for at least a week.

27.   In towns it is advisable to have a number of rallying points or keeps to which isolated parties or individuals should move in the event of being overtaken by airborne attack while away from their units.

28.   In the field also rallying points are useful either pre-arranged or fixed as required. In the latter case a system of whistles or visual signals is recommended, similar to the signals used by German parachutists.

The Immediate Counter Attack

29.   Owing to the vulnerability of the parachutists upon landing, units should be trained to counter attack within fifteen minutes of the landing. Counter attacks later should only be undertaken with strong fire support. The enemy is quick to dig in and will not be dislodged by ill-prepared attacks.

Use of Light Tanks

30.   Light tanks were highly successful in these immediate counter attacks but they must attack before the enemy anti-tank weapons are in position. After delivering their attacks they must be withdrawn and held in reserve to meet further attacks. They should be well dug in and concealed beforehand. Owing to the slow operation of the hand traverse on the turret, it is recommended that tank commanders should be provided with Tommy guns and grenades to enable them to deal with parachutists landing behind them. In the event, revolvers were used with good effect. Many enemy were slow while descending. To deal with snipers, the light tanks covered the area with machine gun fire and then charged and ran over the enemy, finishing him off with revolver or Tommy gun.

31.   Parachutists appear to carry two grenades sewn into the bottom of their trousers. This is important to bear in mind when searching prisoners. As regards gliders, their inmates are most vulnerable before they emerge. Since ammunition is carried in the forepart of the machine, this may prove a profitable target. Grenades are useful after the crew have emerged.

THE DEFENCE OF AERODROMES

32.   The decision as to whether aerodromes should be permanently obstructed or not had been left to General FREYBURG. He decided against permanent obstruction as he hoped to defend them. If effective mining had been possible at the last moment, delay might have been imposed on the enemy but not his ultimate success averted. The question is further discussed under "AIR LESSONS".

33.   Army officers should give tactical advice in siting aerodromes.

34.   It is well to be clear whether the aerodrome is being used operationally by us, in which case aircraft on the ground have to be protected, or whether it has been vacated and only has to be defended against an enemy airborne attack. Although the infantry problem remains the same in either case, the anti-aircraft problem is different. This aspect will be discussed in the anti-aircraft paragraph below.

35.   It is recommended that the aerodrome be defended by two perimeters, an inner and an outer. The role of troops holding the inner perimeter is to bring fire to bear on the aerodrome itself, either against parachutists or aircraft. They must also be able to fire outwards and deal with any parachutists between them and the outer perimeter. The role of troops holding the outer perimeter is to deal with any parachutists landing in their area and broadly to prevent the enemy bringing his mortars within range of the aerodrome, particularly if our own aircraft are still using it. As the German mortar has a range of about 4,000

yards, the outer perimeter should be at least 3,500 yards from the centre of the aerodrome and should include in its garrison mobile troops ready to move out and deal with landings beyond the perimeter. The disposition adopted by Brigadier CHAPPEL at HERAKLION, (vide Map 4) proved very effective.

36. The use of light tanks has been referred to above. It was the intention also on each aerodrome to have two "I" tanks dug in with a view to dealing with landings by enemy troop carriers. In the event troop carriers only landed at MALEME aerodrome and both "I" tanks in that area had broken down beforehand. The effectiveness, therefore, of the "I" tank in this role has still to be proved.

37. The question of field works is discussed below.

38. Field guns and mortars should be sited to bring fire on to the aerodrome, but they must be within the perimeter of infantry defence.

FIELD WORKS

39. The British Army has always been reluctant to dig until compelled to. The air menace has increased the value of field works. A different story might have been told if during the preparatory period strong defence works including well camouflaged concrete pill boxes had been constructed.

40. A difference of opinion exists as to the type of field works best calculated to give protection against bombing. Brigadier CHAPPEL strongly advocated a system of bays, alternate bays having overhead cover. Lieutenant Colonel ANDREWS who was commanding the battalion at MALEME aerodrome advocated the slit trench. He maintained that men were less likely to get buried and that the blast effect of the bomb was better obviated. He also maintained that overhead cover made the men too fond of going to ground. Both have their merits. If time is available probably the system advocated by Brigadier CHAPPEL is best. An enemy constantly flying over the area at 100 or 50 feet may eventually locate slit trenches, when he will attack them individually. If, therefore, they are used, a number of alternatives should be dug, and no effort spared to make them realistic. Dummies should be put inside them. The system of bays has the advantage that the enemy cannot tell in what bay the occupants are. Furthermore, intercommunication is facilitated and this is a major consideration. All are agreed that strong, well camouflaged pill boxes would have been invaluable.

41. The Committee agree with those who advocate the re-introduction of a suitable entrenching tool. In theory the platoon truck brings up the tools, but in the face of complete enemy air superiority it has been shown that movement on roads can be completely paralysed by day. Furthermore, all troops, whether in the front line or the back areas - there is little difference when the enemy can plaster both with his flying machine guns - constantly need to dig in. Many counter attacks failed because the attackers had not the means to dig in and consolidate before being counter attacked and mowed down themselves by machine guns from enemy aircraft.

42.   Field works should not only include trenches and slits. Obstacles of all natures have become increasingly important and the organization and planning of their construction must be tackled on a very much larger scale and with greater vision than is our wont. Beach obstacles against amphibian tanks, road obstacles and obstacles to prevent the landing of enemy aircraft must all be considered. Vast labour will be required and we must be less shy than hitherto in the exploitation of civil labour. British lives are concerned and no half measures can be justified.

CAMOUFLAGE

43.   The value of camouflage under the conditions of this campaign needs no emphasis. Effort and ingenuity in this respect would have been well repaid, particularly in so far as the camouflaging of anti-aircraft gun positions was concerned. This aspect will be developed below.

ANTI-AIRCRAFT DEFENCE

44.   The British soldier lacks cunning. In no field is there more scope than in the layout of anti-aircraft defences. It is realized that if the anti-aircraft gun is to have a $360°$ arc of fire, the question of camouflage becomes difficult, but under the domination of a powerful air force who daily can photograph unmolested our positions, the most strenuous efforts have got to be made to deceive him. Camouflage covers all methods of deception, including the construction of alternative gun pits. These must be dug untiringly. In principle all guns must be mobile and continually moved from one alternative position to another. A proportion of guns should be silent. These in turn must become mobile when they have disclosed their positions.

45.   The layout of the Bofors guns protecting MALEME aerodrome was too orthodox. They were all easily located and if few were destroyed, their teams were neutralized. Gunner N.C.O.s interviewed by the Committee complained that if guns were given a complete $360°$ arc of fire, there was no protection anywhere. While firing at an aircraft to their front there was the continual threat of another one diving at them from behind. It is strongly recommended therefore that part of the arc of fire be reduced so that in principle guns only take on aircraft to their front. This will enable cover to be built over the rear portion of the gun. Guns should be so sited that the blind arc of one is covered by another. In addition to giving a measure of security to the crew that will at least obviate their complete neutralization. Furthermore, it would facilitate camouflage. The Committee also recommend the provision of a shield to give added protection to the team.

46.   For the Bofors gun in particular, too many alternative positions cannot be dug and no effort should be spared to deceive the attacker. The digging of dummy pits and the construction of dummy guns and crews is quite practicable and must be attempted. Mobility again must be aimed at and silent guns should be camouflaged completely.

47.   It should be noted that the original layout of the guns protecting MALEME aerodrome was designed on the assumption that we should be using it and therefore that our aircraft on the ground would have to be protected. Since the effective range of the Bofors is little more than 800 yards, the gun positions were of necessity near the fringe of

the aerodrome, and in consequence, most conspicuous and vulnerable. As soon as we no longer were able to operate from the aerodrome, the role of these guns had changed. Their primary task should then have been to deal with troop carriers trying to land. They would have fulfilled this task much more effectively if they had been disposed irregularly at a distance from the aerodrome.

48. The gun teams were already tired after incessant bombing during the week preceding the attack. The question of reliefs assumed capital importance.

49. All gunners must be armed with rifles or Tommy guns, and gun positions must be within the perimeter of an infantry post. Many casualties were suffered through lack of small arms and through the exposed position of certain guns.

NIGHT OPERATIONS

50. Enemy air superiority virtually paralysed movement on roads by day. Even if movement across country, where cover existed, was possible, intercommunication which entailed the use of roads was only practicable under great difficulty. The successful conduct of an attack was impossible, except for the immediate counter attacks to deal with parachutists. At this moment only were our infantry immune from the constant threat overhead. But the moment was fleeting.

51. Increasing attention should therefore be given to night operations, and any night attacks should be so timed that consolidation and digging in is completed by daylight. If not, the enemy's flying machine guns will mow our infantry down before they are under cover.

52. The fact that the enemy appeared himself to show lack of enterprise at night gives reason to hope that any skill which we can develop in night fighting may produce profitable results. Even bayonet attacks by day were highly successful. By night success should be even greater.

53. It is interesting to note that some units emulated the Greek habit of yelling when they charged. This time-honoured practice was most successful, and provided it is not premature at night, is to be recommended. It is an answer to the whistling dive bomber and the German is probably more susceptible to these psychological tricks than is the British soldier.

ARTILLERY

54. Many of the lessons applicable to anti-aircraft artillery apply equally to field artillery. The ability of the enemy to fly unmolested, skimming the gun positions themselves, will result in very few escaping detection and heavy casualties were suffered. Alternative positions must be dug unceasingly. Camouflage must reach a high standard.

55.	Although comparatively few guns were destroyed, many gun sights were damaged by the bombings and it is recommended that sights be removed except when the guns are actually firing.

LACK OF TRANSPORT

56.	The task of the garrison was complicated in every sphere by lack of transport. From the tactical point of view the relatively small size of the force compared with the size of the island which it was called upon to defend, could only have been compensated for by mobility. This it lacked through want of transport. In the administrative sphere, the vast labour programmes which have been envisaged in this Report could only have been attempted half heartedly without additional transport.

EVACUATION

57.	Experience has almost perfected the procedure for such operations. A few points only need be mentioned.

Need for decentralization.

58.	It would be impossible for a commander successfully to control the rearguard fighting and the organization for evacuation. General FREYBURG therefore wisely entrusted the conduct of the withdrawal to General WESTON.

Necessity for early organization of the beaches

59.	Foresight is necessary if the beach organization is to work smoothly. A few, and only a few, must be constantly planning ahead. If too many are acquainted with the possibility of an eventual evacuation, defeatism may set in. In the event, someone prematurely breathed the word "SPHAKIA". Hundreds beat the gun at the start and broke all records. Confusion therefore set in on the beaches before any organization had been established.

Need for fresh troops to form a bridgehead at the point of embarkation.

60.	The failure of the enemy to land parachutists in the SPHAKIA area has been remarked upon. In the early stages of the withdrawal SPHAKIA was undefended and the troops that eventually arrived were exhausted. If we are again faced with an evacuation problem, it seems reasonable to suppose that the enemy may be more enterprising and may endeavour at an early stage to land parachutists at the point of embarkation. It is therefore strongly recommended that fresh troops are early in position. On occasions it may even be practicable for the Royal Navy to bring them.

Intercommunication between beach and assembly area

61.	It is essential that a good system of intercommunication, preferably by telephone, be organized between the beaches, control posts, assembly areas and rearguard. Guides also in sufficient numbers are essential. Failure to make the most careful arrangements will result in many being left unnecessarily behind.

Necessity for a strong cordon on the beach

62.   On such occasions a number of ill-disciplined men will always be among the first to reach the beaches. Very strong cordons are therefore required close to the actual beaches. These should be supplemented by strong control posts further back.

NAVY LESSONS

DOCKS ORGANIZATION

Port Control Committee

63.   The composition of the Port Control Committee has been given in paragraph 33, Part II, above. The functions of the organization are dealt with in Appendix "A". The following are a few additional Naval points.

64.   As such an organization may again be required, the following are deductions based on the Naval experiences.

65.   The work of the port must be carefully planned. This begins with the question of priorities of unloading for which directions must come from Headquarters. Given priorities, planning can commence. The first requirement is information, which in this case is:-

   (a) Timely warning of the arrival of shipping
   (b) Nature and distribution of cargo
   (c) Loading data of individual ships

To be of any real use this information must be accurate and must be communicated to the Services concerned.

66.   In a port where normal facilities such as cranes, transit sheds and sorting areas do not exist, it is essential that uneconomical loading is accepted. On many occasions stores urgently required were found to be buried under bulk supplies of other natures. Priorities of requirements cannot be laid down for long period ahead as they must vary with the military situation and therefore cargoes must be stowed so that they can be unloaded selectively.

67.   The question of transport on shore is vital to the safety and efficiency of the port. In theory, a vehicle arrives on the quay, is loaded, proceeds to its destination, is unloaded and returns to the quay. Unloading parties at destinations do not normally come under the port organization and during the journey to and from the destination the vehicle is not entirely under the control of the port staff. It is clear therefore that co-operation with the destination staff is essential and rigid control of drivers must be exercised. In addition, consideration must be given to the servicing of vehicles and the relief, feeding and accommodation of the drivers.

68.   Finally, there must be close liaison between the loading and unloading ports, which requires the early arrival of a Sea Transport Officer. At coasting ports where   unloading facilities are non-existent and the servicing and supplying of merchant ships is out of the question, the arrival of a convoy of large heavily loaded ships is most unpopular and hazardous as it is only a question of time before some or all of them are sunk unless air protection can be provided. Ports such as these must not be expected to provide merchant ships with water

and provisions. Labour is a most important question. In the early stages there was a considerable ~~xxx~~ of Greek labour, but as the scale of air attack increased, the supply of this labour decreased. Cypriot labour was employed next but proved unsatisfactory for the same reason. Finally the Australian and New Zealand Brigades supplied a Dock Company which gave excellent service under the most trying conditions.

69.   Action to be taken during air raids is ~~xxx~~ with in Appendix "A".

Hiding of Light Craft

70.   Unloading craft when not in use should be dispersed as widely as possible and if time permits camouflaged "hide-outs" should be constructed for them. At SUDA dispersal was the policy used and we were lucky in not losing any of the landing craft, but one or two motor boats and a caique were destroyed at the same time as the M.T.B.s. The Commander in Chief MEDITERRANEAN has been fully informed of the circumstances under which the M.T.B.s. were destroyed and so it is not proposed to remark on that subject in this paper.

Merchant shipping crews

71.   The control of Merchant shipping crews should be considered. With frequent bombing and machine gunning the crews will not remain in their ships whilst lying in a vulnerable port. The alternatives appear to be:—

(a) The crews to be enrolled into the Navy under some special arrangement. (T.124.)
(b) Place strong military guards on board to force the men to remain in their ships.
(c) Place Service personnel on board for working the ships for unloading and for their security.

EVACUATION

Beach organization

72.   The need for good communication between the beaches and assembly areas has been touched upon above. An officer should be appointed with full knowledge of the local situation on shore to act as Beachmaster. He should get in touch with the Naval Beachmaster as soon as he lands and co-operate with him during the embarkation.

Numbers to be embarked.

73.   To ensure an orderly embarkation the figures given by the Naval C. in C. must be the basis on which to work and these figures should not be exceeded, it being understood that the maximum number of available ships will be sent and that each ship will be allowed to embark the maximum number of men, taking into consideration the conditions under which they have got to withdraw.

CAMOUFLAGE

74.   The camouflage and disguise of Merchant ships does not appear to have been considered in any detail so far during this war.

CONCLUDING REMARKS

1.   The planning of operations such as the defence of CRETE demands exceptional foresight and the most intimate co-operation between the Services if due weight is to be given to the many factors involved. The Committee are of opinion that until the eleventh hour no Service gave due weight to the preponderating factor affecting this problem, which was the overwhelming superiority of the German Air Force.

2.   The campaigns in NORWAY, FRANCE and GREECE had produced a wealth of lessons; they had been ill-digested. Committees also have sat, but their labours appear to have been in vain.

3.   The Army will not soon forget the help rendered at great sacrifice by the Royal Navy during these difficult days; nor will it forget the valiant struggle which a handful of young pilots were asked to face against an overwhelming enemy air force.

APPENDIX "A"

ADMINISTRATIVE NARRATIVE

PART I. (October 1940 up till the arrival of W Force)

1.   The development of the maintenance problem in CRETE has been treated in chronological order. A short description of the work done by certain services during the period is also given.

2.   On 28.10.40 SUDA BAY was selected as being the advanced re-fuelling base by C-in-C Mediterranean, certain troops were despatched for its protection, and the following scales of reserves were laid down for the force:

Supplies	45 days
Amn. except A.A.	45 days at F.F.C. wastage rate
Amn. A.A.	550 r.p.g. with unit)
	650 " reserve) Hy
	400 r.p.g. with unit) Lt.
	15,200 rds reserve)
Petrol	30 days at 4 galls per day per vehicle

3.   On 2.11.40 the maintenance reserves were ordered to be increased to a total of 90 days, the Force Commander being authorized to buy locally supplies and M.T. and to arrange for the assistance of local labour as required.

4.   On 8.11.40 the maintenance reserve figure was reduced to 60 days.

5.   On 9.11.40 a report was received from CRETE that progress in development was hindered by lack of civilian labour and civilian transport.

6.   On 12.11.40 a questionnaire was despatched to CRETE demanding information in regard to water, cold storage, fresh meat, local supplies, labour and acommodation. It was noted that answers must depend largely on tactical considerations, and a discussion with the B.G.S., who was in CRETE, was advised.

7.   On 14.11.40 the W.O. were informed that "a small force is quite sufficient for CRETE at present and larger force would cause inconvenient and unnecessary commitment from both military and naval point of view."

8.   On 10.11.40 an estimated labour shortage of all services of 800 was reported, and military parties were used to help unload ships.

9.   On 31.12.40 as a result of a personal visit by D.Q.M.G. ALMYRO, CANDIA and ALIKIANU were reported as areas suitable for the reception of one Bde Gp to each area, and complete plans for the first two areas were to be drawn up immediately. In the event of troops being placed at CANDIA, the necessary reserves could be placed there with them, but the main base would remain at SUDA.

10.   On 29.1.41 General Gambier Parry forwarded a report agreeing with 1st Key plan on the assumption that one of his roles was to establish a Base Area for a force of one Division in the Area SUDA BAY-CANEA, and emphasized the need for more M.T.

11.   On 15.4.41 General Weston forwarded a report stating his intention to establish two main defended areas at SUDA and HERAKLION demanding further aerodromes for the construction of which the R.A.F. were responsible.

12.   By 16.4.41 stocks were 60 days for 20,000 for everything except ammunition and petrol, and on that date an increase to 30,000 was ordered.

13.   On 18.4.41 orders were issued for the stocking on a basis of 30,000 for 90 days with supplies, P.O.L., Tentage scale A., blankets 2 per man, K.D. and reserve of cookers, cooking utensils, water bottles and water containers. Maximum use was to be made of unit transport. Supplies and essential R.E. Stores were also to be delivered to HERAKLION, and requirements in Defence stores were to be submitted by G. No P. and L. units were to be despatched, but Naval Landing Coy and unit labour to be used.

14.   On 21.4.41 two additional Q staff officers and representatives from the services were sent to CRETE to assist in organising the reception of troops from GREECE. On 25.4.41 a Q Liaison Officer was also despatched from G.H.Q., M.E.

15.   On 27.4.41 reconnaissance of the southern posts was ordered. Field Depots were to be disposed, with supplies and P.O.L., in areas in which troops were stationed. A report on Greek requirements was also called for.

16.   On 6.5.41 the following M.N.B.D.O. vehicles arrived in CRETE:

8 cwt.	24	Ambulances	5	Staff cars	2
15 cwt.	15	3-ton lorries	10	Recovery trailers	1
Matadors	10	W/Shop "	2	M/Cs.	50
Gun transporters	2	S/L trailers	3		

In addition, the following vehicles were despatched:

S.T.		O.S.	
Lorries	94	15 cwt	86
Amb. cars	6	Bren carriers	60
		M/Cs	76

17.   The following stores were despatched to CRETE:- to increase reserve above 60 days for 20,000

	Arrived Tons	Turned back as could not be unloaded. Tons	Sunk Tons
P.O.L.		15,000	
Supplies	920	(2,480 (1,980	1,580
Ammunition	600	400	436
O.S. Stores	368	638	842
R.E. Stores	812	1,125	545

18. **Works.** 42 Fd Coy R.E. was included in the first order of battle. As no C.R.K. Works accompanied the original force, the following tasks were undertaken by the unit, assisted by local labour: Development of roads in the Dock, Base and Defence Areas, the laying of the Decauville railway from the Docks to CANEA, and the erection of steel hutting in the B.O.D. and B.S.D.

Assistance was given in building defence works at HERAKLION. There was no scarcity of unskilled labour for this work. Base Depots were planned on the basis of one Division to be ready by end March.

19. **Medical.** Medical reconnaissances were made in Nov. of all areas on the island that were likely to prove malarial, and work on draining, ditching and later oiling was started in February. Trained inspectors and gangs were brought over from GREECE, and were still working when the island was evacuated. As a result of this work cases of malaria were very few.

20. **Movement Control.** As a result of the small amount of tonnage to be moved into CRETE, no Docks personnel were despatched there, and Movement Control organized and supervised all port working. As Greek conscription for military service increased, assistance had to be sought to augment the skilled local labour available, and Arab stevedores were accordingly despatched.

Tonnages into HERAKLION were dealt with by local personnel completely.

No S.T.O. staff arrived in the island until 19 April.

PART 2. (After the arrival of W Force up till the withdrawal)

1. General State of the Garrison at the Outset

The original garrison of one Inf. Bde. plus some C.D. and A.A. tps and small ancillary services were more or less equipped to W.E. scales. The reinforcements of M.N.B.D.O., two regular Bns. and Layforce elements arrived with G.1098 equipment but M.N.B.D.O. was actually the only formation which brought any transport at all with it, with the exception of a few trucks.

The bulk of the garrison was made up of W Force troops which by force of Naval circumstances had arrived from GREECE in CRETE instead of EGYPT. From the point of view of readiness for war in CRETE the best of these W. Force troops were N.Z. and Australian Inf. Bns. which had succeeded in bringing with them practically all their rifles and Bren guns, some A.T. rifles and a few M.Gs., some without tripods. The best equipped of these men had a greatcoat and their personal equipment.

However, many of even these infantry men had not got greatcoats or personal equipment. No unit had any unit equipment whatsoever or any transport. This meant that even in these best W.Force units for example many men had to cook their food in some kind of ration tin having no mess tin, and eat it with their fingers until they improvised or borrowed a spoon or fork. The worst equipped W Force men had nothing at all except some form of clothing. Moreover, a large proportion of these W Force men were sappers, gunners and members of all ancillary services as well as Cypriots and Palestinian A.M.P.C. elements. Some of these were led by their officers and in some cases by more or less complete unit H.Qs, but a considerable number were leaderless and remained so for a considerable time. Many were armed with rifles - some had personal equipment but some only a bandolier of S.S.A. Even some of the best formed of these W. Force elements necessarily arrived in small parties or as individuals; some had even been shipwrecked on the way.

As regards reception, H.Q. CREFORCE had done the best they could, considering they had no transport available, no stocks of unit equipment, only a few accommodation stores and no personnel available to staff reception camps. They had selected areas where there was water and olive tree cover to which all arrivals were directed to make their way on foot. The first of these was about 2 miles from SUDA port where hot tea and tinned rations were obtainable. Thence men were directed on to separate areas for Australians, N.Z. and other British troops.

It was naturally therefore rare to find formed bodies of men led along the road to their appropriate camps by their own officers. In general it was a stream of tired human beings wanting to rest and recuperate from the last conditions in GREECE and in many cases with a tendency to "windiness" vis-a-vis observation by enemy aircraft. In a proportion of cases of the toughest and least trained men, there was an active revulsion against military discipline and advantage was taken of the opportunities offered to avoid being brought under control. In consequence, for the first 10 days at least, there were a number of men at large, many armed with rifles, living as tramps in the hills and olive groves.

2. Immediate steps taken to improve conditions

Camp staffs were appointed; in the case of British camps these were from among artillery units from W Force for whom there were then no guns. Appeal was made to all original CREFORCE units to hand in as much as they could of their cook pots, etc. on the principle that all troops should have their share of what there was. The scale of blankets was reduced from three to one per man, and in this way, sufficient were just obtainable for every man to have one.

The problem of bringing all loose elements under control however, was much more difficult, largely owing to the impossibility of giving the military police any transport for rounding up. A curfew for troops at 1800 hrs daily was introduced in the SUDA-CANEA area, and it was promulgated that all men not in formed units or camp control would be treated as deserters. Moreover, the gradual organization of some gunners into gunner units, and of others into improvised units armed with rifles helped to clear things up. Everything possible was done to simplify the procedure for disposing of serious cases amongst N.Z., Australian and other troops respectively. However, even F.G.C.M. procedure proved very slow.

A census was taken of every vehicle in the island. Unit transport particularly in the case of original CREFORCE units, A.A. & C.D. and M.N.D.B.O. was reduced to the minimum laid down by the G.S. Vehicles so thrown up, driven by unit personnel, were placed in a composite R.A.S.C. company, to provide a pool for port clearance, and for troop carrying of a reserve Inf. Bde. This was achieved with difficulty, and not fully. For port clearance, anything up to 40 lorries daily was really required. This number was seldom available because other priority requirements such as moving guns and ammunition by road had so often to be ruled as essential by the G.S. Moreover, as was only natural, units parted with their vehicles with great reluctance. For the first fortnight the commanders of the MALEME and RETIMO sectors could not even be provided with a vehicle each for their sole use.

3. Evacuation of surplus personnel

The policy was to get rid as soon as possible of all surplus personnel to ease the maintenance problem as much as for any other reason. Some were despatched to EGYPT but not as many as was desired at the outset. To some extent this was due to lack of escorted shipping and partly to a fair proportion being equipped with guns or turned into improvised rifle units. Opportunities were missed in the early part of this period, when reception was the main concern.

4. Strengths to be maintained

As a result the total strength of British troops to be maintained remained till the end in the region of 30,000 although the fighting strength was actually less than that of a division at W.E. and equipment and transport for even the fighting portion of the force was lacking.

In addition, there were the following to be maintained:-

Greek Army	14,000
Prisoners of War	15,000
Greek population	400,000

It was apparent at the outset that all the needs of these must be imported through the medium of one machine and that, although there might be committees to discuss details of needs, "Q" Branch Force H.Q. would have to act in a most direct manner with G.H.Q., M.E. if there was to be any hope of a successful solution of the problems.

The Greek Army had no transport, practically no arms or equipment and no resources of food at all. In fact they were merely recruit units and there was no organization. A successful meeting was held between the D.A. & Q.M.G. and the Greek Army Chief of Staff, as a result of which a simple organization of Greek Army ancillary services was to result. The A.Q.M.G. of 27 B.M.M. was to become A.Q.M.G. with the Greek Army and to have to help him two officers of S.T., Ordnance and Medical Services as well as a "Q" Movement and Docks officer to assist in port clearance and Food distribution system.

This British staff was to act in respect of the needs of the Greek civil population as well as the Greek Army. Unfortunately as the harvest was not yet gathered in, the food situation of the civil population was at its worst. To add to the difficulties there was no effective civil government and therefore no organization for clearance of food landed at SUDA or for efficient distribution throughout the island. Moreover, all civil M.T. and nearly all animals had been requisitioned by the Greek Government for the campaign on the mainland.

The Prisoners of War were naturally on rather short rations.

As a result, from the outset it was necessary to give some food to put heart into the eight Greek bns. actually employed in sectors, and to the Prisoners of War who had been transferred to CRETE by the Greek military authorities.

Maintenance System

5. It was neither feasible nor desirable to alter the layout of the main base depots which were largely Decauville served, well dispersed and concealed in dumps in the olive groves close to SUDA PORT.

These contained roughly 30 days balanced rations for 30,000 men plus a certain quantity of unbalanced items, some S.A.A. but little else.

Immediately W Force H.Q. was organized on 1/2 May and the General distribution of troops decided, steps were taken to establish F.S.Ds of approx 15 days' rations and P.O.L. in proportion, for the strengths in the outlying sectors of HERAKLION, Central (RETIMO - GEORGOPOULOS) and MALEME - GALATOS.

The location of these in sectors was left to Sector Commanders, but it was laid down that each unit must hold 3 days' rations in addition to the F.S.D. stocks, and that anything in excess of this held by units would be in diminution of F.S.D. stocks.

All ammunition and all defence stores were allocated to Sectors as and when they arrived, and except in the last stages, when some .303 was accumulated, there were practically no stocks retained in Ordnance or R.E. Depots.

The detail of distribution of ammunition and defence stores was left to the G.S. to arrange with the A.D.O.S. and C.E. in detail "Q" Branch only holding a watching brief and anticipating possible needs by demands on G.H.Q.

The first German parachute attack included the landing of some gliders astride the main CANEA-SUDA road, so that access to the main base depots was partially denied. In consequence, when the situation was cleaned up, F.S.Ds of rations, P.O.L. and ammunition were established also in the outskirts of CANEA itself, where they would be readily accessible for distribution by road East or West.

Every effort was made to utilize local resources, but these were limited practically to supply of vegetables, some fruit and the baking of bread.

6. Medical Stores

Throughout the short campaign, there was an acute shortage of medical stores, due to previous enemy sinkings. The proportion of killed was low, but the rate of comparatively serious and walking wounded cases was high.

7. Welfare

In addition to shortages of essential equipment for cooking, etc. and other hardships, there was also the complete lack of amenities for the troops.

E.F.I. stores soon ran out of some of the main essentials, such as cigarettes, whisky and beer. There was no English literature in the island except the Force H.Q. newspaper provided with the greatest difficulty.

Under such conditions, a few amenities, such as cigarettes, beer, reading matter and footballs are essential as a restorative of morale.

8. SUDA PORT Clearance

Especially after experience in GREECE it was obvious from the outset that there was grave danger of air attack drastically restricting the tonnage which could be cleared through SUDA.

Immediate steps were therefore taken to warn G.H.Q. of the possibility, to put some A.A. defence at HERAKLION and to recce the Southern beaches from the point of view of immediate use or possible development. In addition, complete lists were forwarded to G.H.Q. by special hand giving full details of all essentials for the British and Greek Armies as well as the civil population.

There were necessarily based on a modest programme of building up 15 days' reserve by 1 June, 22 days by 15 June, and 30 days by 1 July.

All non-essentials such as tentage were ruthlessly cut out.

The tonnage cleared through SUDA was for several days worked up to at least 700 tons a day, working by day in the face of some enemy air attack that came usually each evening by aircraft based on GREECE. There was, however, a perpetual shortage of transport and the other usual difficulties arising out of use of a port not constructed for dealing with such tonnage, with no shore facilities at all, such as cranes, etc., a marked shortage of lighters and no real ship repair facilities.

As in GREECE the widespread air alarm by means of syrens was most detrimental to the working of the port, and finally such air alarms in the port were abolished on the principle of continuing work until actual air attack took place. However, at a later stage, the scale and suddenness of dive bombing attack became so great that the presence of enemy aircraft in the neighbourhood resulted in the stoppage of work.

Resort was made to night work, but in the absence of an elaborate well-organized system this cannot be expected to yield the same results as day working. In particular, a large proportion of the ships being discharged were damaged by hits or near misses, and in nearly every case their engines ceased to function. As they had no ancillary engines in working order for winches, and as there was no separate lighting system, power had to be provided by putting a tug or other small ship alongside.

Moreover, the ships' civil crews abandoned their ships and military winchmen and stevedores found great difficulty in organizing their work in the dark without the crew's assistance.

There were also the problems of slow turn round of N.T. in the depots as well as in the port, guards, and military police, hot tea and meals for labour, stevedores and transport drivers, organization of P.A.D. trenches and medical arrangments, fire fighting squads, etc. etc.

In SUDA, as formerly in PIRAEUS, it was found necessary to appoint a combatant Lt. Col. without an office, to supervise in the port area without interfering with the technical working. He did, however, attend the daily conference between the Naval and Military port staffs.

9. Supply to Sectors

To the greatest possible extent, supply to Sectors was made by sea rather than by road, owing to the desperate shortage of transport. This alternative gradually fell away in capcity. Greek crews would not man their ships or caiques. It was difficult to get hold of sound caiques. Lighters broke down and were sunk. Volunteer military crews were called for and some actually employed.

10. Southern Beaches

TYMBAKI and KASTELLI were the only places in the South coast served by N.T. road. Owing to enemy action TIMBAKI could only serve the HERAKLION sector, and SELINOS KASTELLI was rendered inaccessible. The rapid construction of M.T. roads to other beaches, notably SPHAKIA, was not possible. SPHAKIA was more or less typical of the South coast of CRETE. The road ended at the top of an escarpment leaving 7 miles to the coast to be traversed by hilly mule track.

However, even had any other Southern beaches been served by M.T. road, the difficulties of provision of A.A. defence, lighters and M.T. remained.

11. Development of the acute maintenance situation.

To meet all essential current needs and to build up reserves it was decided to aim at a clearance of 30,000 tons a month, although it was recognized that some 20,000 might have to suffice. The first G.H.Q. plan with C-in-C Med. was to have a fortnightly convoy, but this was strongly advised against by W Force, who put forward a plan for clearing through SUDA weekly two fastish ships of 2,500 tons each, with an additional specially loaded one fortnightly to be cleared at HERAKLION chiefly for Greek needs. When the loss of shipping at SUDA became acute, A.A. defence was concentrated in an umbrella over the pier and quay.

However, it soon became evident that maintenance through SUDA WITH THE type of ships available was not possible. The only alternative was a daily delivery of small quantities by fast ships getting in, discharging and getting away under cover of darkness. For this, neither the ships nor escorts were available, and for M.T. delivery it was not a feasible proposition. As a last resort, G.H.Q., M.E. planned to run one convoy of three ships ashore in SUDA BAY, relying on night clearance and on fire fighting squads to prevent their destruction by burning. It is very doubtful whether this would have been successful in sufficient degree to warrant the experiment. In the count SUDA BAY had to be abandoned to the enemy before it could be tried.

PART W (The withdrawal and final evacuation)
Maintenance in the last stages

The HERAKLION sector never ran short of food and were successfully given some ammunition and medical stores by air. The RETIMO sector ran short of both, food and ammunition. In spite of every effort this situation was not relieved, owing to a small enemy post astride the road just East of RETIMO town. Several attempts at air dropping apparently failed, and in spite of every effort by the Naval Staff attempted delivery by caiques and lighters also failed.

In the SUDA-MALEME area, maintenance of food and ammunition was all right until the very last stage, when the sudden large scale withdrawal with evacuation from SPHAKIA as the objective precluded adequate preparation. With the exceptions as stated below, some transport was used for carrying back wounded, and no supplies or stores were cleared back from SUDA.

The last consignment of supplies and ammunition delivered by warship to SUDA was cleared to NEON KHORION which was the first planned withdrawal staging area. To this place also some rations and P.O.L. were despatched from the Depots, but the failure of M.T. to return to control of the R.A.S.C. transport organization, and the rapidity of the withdrawal through the Base Depot Area near SUDA BAY, made it impossible to form any F.S.Ds. further South on the SPHAKIA road from stocks existing in the North or delivered at SUDA.

It was hoped that all withdrawing fighting troops would bring back 3 days' rations with them. This they largely did, although the situation was aggravated by the shortage of biscuits, and the impossibility of continuing the supply of bread in lieu.

The last alternative was to get supplies ashore at SPHAKIA from the ships arriving to evacuate personnel. In the first instance, 15,000 rations were asked for in this manner, but it is believed that the quantity of essentials of balanced rations was not delivered.

Clearance from the beach 7 miles uphill to the fighting troops had to be done by soldiers, exhausted ill-organized men actually awaiting evacuation.

Finally, air dropping was arranged, but with little success, owing, presumably, to the terrain and the failure of recognition signals.

APPENDIX "A"

Administrative Lessons.

GENERAL

1.	The conditions under which the battle was fought are again emphasized.

With the exception of very few of the troops engaged, the majority of them had arrived in CRETE with no stores, ammunition, tools or transport. Reserves held on the island were not sufficient to provide for all their needs. Owing to complete enemy air supremacy, any form of movement or activity by day was impossible. These exceptional circumstances must therefore be borne in mind throughout.

2.	The possible lessons that may be learned have been divided into the three main phases:

       X. Immediately prior to the battle.
       Y. During the battle and withdrawal.
       Z. During the evacuation.

Phase X. Immediately prior to the Battle

Port and Base Areas.

3.	During this period, the port of SUDA, through which the maintenance of the main force was being done, was constantly harassed by the enemy air, as was the Base Area to the southwest of the port. The normal unloading of ships was therefore practically impossible, and discharge had to be effected with maximum speed, in order to keep the period during which the ships were subjected to air attack to a minimum.

To ensure the rapid and efficient turn round of shipping, berthed on a programme previously agreed by the Naval and Military authorities, an organization dealing with the following must be set up by the Base Commandant:

    (a) Air Raid look-out system linked with P.A.D. measures such as trenches, medical, policy for ships' crews, etc.

    (b) Supervision of turn round of M.T. in the Docks and Base areas, guards and police in ships and in the Docks area, and the distribution of labour to the best advantage.

    (c) Fire fighting and mine spotting.

    (d) Welfare of the men working in the Docks area.

4.	In CRETE it was found that the placing of responsibility for all the points in the hand of one senior army officer, produced the best results. When dealing with such matters as guards in ships, he would naturally consult the Naval authorities.

5.	Establishment of Port Control Committee

In addition to the appointment of the officer referred to in para 4 above, it is considered necessary to form at the earliest possible moment a Port Control Committee consisting of the following:

King's Harbourmaster
S.T.O.
N.O. i/c Local Craft
Docks Service
Movement Control
Reps. of R.A.F., Services and P. and L.
Allied Liaison Officer (if necessary)

6. Shipping and Port Clearance

In order to ensure rapid turn round and discharge of shipping the following suggestions are made:

(a) If possible, Docks Operating Coy. should function at the Port from the outset. Reliance should not be placed on local labour operating under Movement Control.

(b) All ships should arrive with copies of stowage plans. These should be prepared at the port of loading by the S.T.O. staff in conjunction with the ship's officers while loading is being done. This may facilitate the rapid tracing of any stores urgently demanded during unloading.

(c) Every possible form of rapid labour saving facility is required; small mechanical hoists and gravity runways both for ships and lighters; inches should be operated by engines with their own power source, and portable or battery lighting apparatus is required in the event of the failure of the main power supply.

(d) Small craft for ferrying personnel or for use as lighters are essential. Motor launches capable of towing the small craft must be provided.

(e) Every port should have some fire fighting apparatus for use from a tug or lighter.

(f) Shipping repair facilities were reported as being necessary in discharge ports.

(g) During the reconnaissance of the port, special note should be taken of handling gear, gangways, ladders, hoses and available water. All ships should carry additional ladders for use in holds, and extra gear of which the port is stated to be deficient.

(h) Consideration might be given to the cutting of extra openings in the sides of ships so that they could be worked at night with hatch covers on and lights burning in the holds. Assisted by gravity runways, the speed of discharge of certain easily handled stores like ammunition could be increased.

(i) The use of prime movers and trailers is suggested as a more rapid and economical method of port clearance as opposed to lorries. Prime movers and trailers have many advantages over the 3 ton or 10 ton lorry. They are easily shipped in the first instance to the port, and present no craneage difficulties. With the sides removed the trailer take up very little hold space. Working three sets of trailers to each prime mover, both the Docks area and the Base area could be worked with a minimum dead period. The loss of trailers from enemy action is not so serious as the loss of lorry units. If the prime mover is destroyed or is out of action, it can always be replaced by a lorry.

6. **Ship clearance under conditions of enemy air supremacy**

When the enemy possesses air supremacy it will probably not be possible to rely on one area for discharge, and these additional conditions must be fulfilled:

(a) Smaller and faster ships will have to be employed and every effort made to clear their cargoes during the hours of darkness.

(b) It may be necessary to land supplies at scattered points on beaches. To enable this to be done, suitable lighters or landing craft will have to be provided. Craft of the M.L.C. type are preferable. These craft will have to be camouflaged and hidden by day, clear of the beaches on which the stores and supplies have been discharged.

(c) The amount of tonnage that can be dealt with by this means is limited and this method could only supply the most urgent needs of a force.

(d) In CRETE the use of the southern beaches was the only alternative to SUDA and HERAKLION. The extent to which they could have been used was limited by the lack of transport and of roads serving the beaches and connecting up with the main defensive sectors in the north.

(e) Once the Germans had secured air bases from which they could operate dive bombers unopposed, it became impossible to keep any shipping in any harbour or at any beach in CRETE during the hours of daylight. Some degree of A.A. protection would have been necessary at the beaches had they been used, failing which all uncleared stores would have been destroyed. SUDA and HERAKLION were the only places that could offer any degree of A.A. protection.

(f) In order to ensure that transport and labour ashore is awaiting the arrival of lighters at the correct beaches and times, the closest liaison between the Naval and Military authorities must be maintained.

(g) If rapid discharge of cargo is to be secured under these conditions, careful loading at the port of embarkation is essential. Every care must be taken to ensure that only vital stores and supplies are despatched.

(h) As an alternative, the use of train ferry type ships filled with loaded M.T. is suggested. These ships are fast, possess big carrying capacity, draw comparatively little water and could have been used on a beach like SPHAKIA where the prow could have cleared the shallow water. Supplies of netting and pegs could be carried in the ship. The discharge of these loaded lorries could be done very rapidly, and if required their places could be taken by empty ones driven on board.

7. **Establishment of Field Supply Depots**

As soon as the defences of the island were placed on a sector basis, F.S.Ds. were established in these sectors, a small central reserve being left in the Base Area.

The formation of these F.S.Ds. in any defended area is a necessary step, because the method of German attack appears to follow a definite sequence adopted both in GREECE and in CRETE:-

    (a) The destruction of ports and quays and the sinking of ships, thus preventing the reinforcement of men and material by sea.

    (b) The gaining of air superiority.

    (c) The destruction of M.T. parks, petrol dumps, and supply depots.

    (d) The bombing of Ordnance store depots. Ammunition dumps and depots were not attacked.

    (e) The machine-gunning and bombing of roads and communications, making transport of material or movement of personnel extremely difficult and costly.

8.   Composition of F.S.Ds.

F.S.Ds. should contain the following supplies and stores:

Rations in men days.
P.O.L. in vehicle miles.
A.G.O.
Ammunition by nature by rounds.
Anti-tank mines.
Tools.
Barbed wire and pickets.
Sandbags.
Medical stores.

The amount of ammunition and Defence Stores held in any sector must depend on the allocation made by G.

Inflammable items should be stored separately. In one instance, a complete medical store dump was destroyed as a result of ether being set on fire.

9.   Marking of F.S.Ds.

It is necessary that these F.S.D. should be notified, clearly marked, adequately guarded, easily found, and laid out on the ground, so that a maximum amount of supplies or stores may be picked up either by marching infantry or by M.T. parties in a minimum space of time. Within the depot there should be several dispersed dumps containing a complete variety of the supplies and stores held by the Depot. By this system, rapid loading is ensured, and the danger of the complete destruction of any one commodity by air bombing minimized. Alternatively, the depot should be organized into sub-depots, manned by the service concerned in each case. East sub-depot would have dispersed dumps.

10. Issues to Units

In the case of every unit, an immediate issue of three days' supplies was ordered and this was intended as a unit reserve. Issues in excess of this were left to the discretion of Sector Commanders. General ammunition was also issued to units in large quantities.

In addition to these reserves, daily maintenance was to a certain extent successful from D.I.Ds. which had already been established. Once the main attack had been launched, the lack of transport, the inability to move in M.T. by day, and sniping by night by parties of parachutists who had escaped being mopped up, rendered normal methods impossible. For this reason therefore, large quantities of ammunition need to be held by such units as A.A. batteries. If alternative positions are prepared, ammunition should be dumped and concealed at every position.

11. Early preparation of Administration Plan

Even if the G plan is not fully prepared, Q must make arrangements to meet possible eventualities.

In CRETE the centrally placed road SPHAKIA - NEON KHORION was a possible line of withdrawal, or a probable line of communication if we were forced to abandon using SUDA as a base port. For these reasons it is considered that F.S.D. might have been established on the line of this road to correspond with the possible tactical lay backs.

Had there been no necessity for a withdrawal, these F.S.Ds. could have been drawn on in the ordinary course of maintenance.

The provision of these dumps would have ensured supply to at least some troops using this road in a withdrawal.

Only one such dump was established at NEON KHORION, of whose existence many units were unaware, though desperately in need of food. When the Germans overran it there were still supplies untouched. It is admitted that this method entails putting supplies and stores on the ground, a system which is not economical in transport, labour or supplies, but it is considered that where there is any likelihood of the enemy obtaining air supremacy great dispersion to ensure rapid supply to units is necessary.

Until the G plan for withdrawal has been outlined, any detailed plan by Q cannot be made, and the delay in producing this outline plan made an administrative plan difficult to put into operation at such short notice.

PHASE Y. During the battle and withdrawal

12. Withdrawal of Administrative Units

Once it is agreed that a withdrawal is necessary, the sending back with a minimum of delay of administrative units not essential to the conduct of the withdrawal should be ordered. These units are difficult to replace, and everything possible to ensure their safe removal should be done.

This withdrawal must be on a planned and timed programme to ensure that it is orderly and completely under control.

If the enemy has complete air superiority, movement must be by night.

Preliminary reconnaissance of lying up areas for administrative units must be thorough, unit areas being allotted so that they remain a formed body, each under its own officers.

The ability to withdraw administrative troops in this way is dependent on an early decision from G.

13. Provost

During the withdrawal and at the assembly area north of the beaches, the need for adequate traffic control and provost organization was felt.

To ensure that transport is not misappropriated and that the withdrawal is at all times under control, a definite plan for stragglers' posts, walking wounded collecting posts and traffic control posts must be put into execution.

It is considered that, had this been done, much transport could have been collected and sent back into the battle area, and used by the fighting troops at night to increase their mobility and to assist in the general withdrawal plan.

It is necessary that control posts be sited in depth along the line of withdrawal.

All Provost personnel must be adequately mobile. In this particular withdrawal it was considered that something stronger than Stragglers' Posts was required to reorganize many of the troops who were withdrawing.

PHASE Z. Maintenance during the evacuation

14. Once the enemy had overrun the F.S.D. at NEON KHORIAON the sources of supply were reduced to the rations that each individual man carried and to the dump that had been established on the beach at SPHAKIA.

Owing to the complete absence of transport which had been left at the end of the unfinished road no forward supply to rearguard units was possible. Carrier parties were organized but very few of the men were strong enough to do the journey up the hill with supplies while some went straight off to the cave area with their load.

Emergency supplies such as those at SPHAKIA must be carefully selected. In this case sacks of flour had been included. The contents of these sacks were used for camouflaging the dump. The need for adequate provost and for an issuing organization at dumps and water points under similar conditions is emphasized.

GENERAL LESSONS

15. Tentage

Only when climatic conditions make it absolutely necessary, should tentage be issued for forward troops. It should then be restricted to the two man bivouac tent.

When troops move forward, this tentage should be left and collected later as Salvage. Transport for moving tentage should not be permanently allotted to units.

16. Transport

Except for senior commanders for long distance work, the truck should replace the staff car, thereby providing a further general utility vehicle and easing the maintenance problem. Unit transport should be reduced, thereby freeing more for a general pool system.

This necessitates a revision of G. 1098 equipment. Forward units should carry only absolute essentials and reserves of stores should be cut to a minimum. Trailers carrying eight stretchers with a canvas roof were suggested.

17. Cooking Facilities

The Coy cooker unit was reported on by several units as being an impractical method of cooking food for forward troops as detailed distribution was found to be most difficult. A Primus stove per section was recommended. When troops are on reserve, additional facilities could be issued.

Rations

18. Operational scale

It is considered that a scale for active operations should be drawn up and only those items which are reasonably certain of being used should be included.

The necessity for cutting transport down to a minimum and the probable resultant lack of the full scale of unit cooking equipment makes it necessary only to include in this scale items that are suitable for use under all circumstances.

19. Packing

These items should be packed in a composite form, say, 12 men's rations for one day in one case. This admits of easy and safe handling and distribution and reduces the bulk from the transport point of view.

20. Emergency scale

In addition it is suggested that an Emergency ration be provided which should embody the following qualities:-

(i) Each man should be able to carry enough for three days.

(ii) Be a non-thirst producer. The present ration is not suitable from this point of view.

The use of tablets require hard specialized training and is therefore as a general solution not considered satisfactory.

21. E.F.I.

It is considered that in the forward areas no service should be provided but that for troops in reserve every effort should be made to provide them with Canteen facilities. At the same time the shipping overseas to an expeditionary force of such items as beer should be eliminated. Drinks in the form of powders should be sold.

22. Clothing

Shorts were adversely criticised, and K.D. trousers were advocated. The turned up shorts are apt to chafe the leg. A strong material not so closely woven as the present K.D. was suggested. A hot weather kit as under was put forward for consideration:-

Cotton Vest
Flannel shirt, cut square and worn outside the trousers by day.
K.D. trousers
Anklets
Cardigans
Greatcoats

The present steel helmet when at all worn, is very visible from the air. This fact was reported by the Germans.

For winter wear, serge battle dress is excellent. The forage cap should be replaced by a soft round cap or beret, carried in the haversack when the steel helmet is worn.

Supply of Machine Guns

23.   Machine guns must be sent from EGYPT complete in one package, so that they may be sent forward similarly packed. Instances in GREECE occurred of Bren guns arriving but no magazines. In CRETE Vickers M.G. were unloaded but the tripods eventually went down with the ship.

Medical

24.   Water

Under the conditions that existed in CRETE, where drinking water had to be drawn from wells, and there, generally speaking, the water discipline was poor, it is suggested that individual water sterilising tablets should be issued to every man.

25.   Malaria, Tetanus, etc.

Prophylactic treatment and other precautions proved their value, and as a result of them very little malaria, typhoid, tetanus, etc. was reported.

26.   Marking of Hospitals and Hospital Ships

The Red Cross on 7 General Hospital was reported as being visible at 15,000 ft. but it was savagely attacked from the air. The hospital at KNOSSOS being clear of any military area was left untouched. The Germans stated themselves that if wounded men move in a formed body with no steel helmets and displaying a large red cross flag, such columns will not be attacked from the air. This statement was shown to be correct in one instance.

It is considered that the Red Cross on Hospital Ships should be more clearly marked, and that if possible these ships should be loaded well clear of any other shipping. It was reported that when this was done in CRETE, they were not attacked, although the hospital ship was bombed on the way to EGYPT.

27.   Stretchers.

It is considered that in forward hospitals that are likely to be bombed or machine gunned hospital beds should not be provided.

The patient is too exposed to bomb splinters and lies more quietly and happily if placed on a stretcher on the ground. The abolition of hospital beds also does away with the need for mattresses, thereby producing a substantial saving in shipping space.

28.   Dropping of Ammunition from the Air

When ammunition was dropped from the air with no parachute it was stated that .303 was in serviceable condition when retrieved, but Tommy Gun Ammunition was very badly damaged. Dropping in shallow water was suggested as a possible solution.

Supply Dropping

29.   As a result of the success that attended the German method of supply dropping from the air, it is considered that this method should be carefully studied. Full details are contained in the R.A.F. portion of this report.

30. Entrenching tools

As a result of the lack of tools (At Maleme 22 Bn. only had 8 shovels and 9 picks) the necessity for the individual entrenching tool was felt. The German tool was most favourably reported on.

31. Labour

The difficulties encountered in CRETE emphasized the absolute necessity of ensuring that Pioneer and Labour Coys, are officered by young fully trained men and that the British N.C.Os. are in every way comparable to those in other units. These companies should be armed and drilled so that they possess the ability to use their weapons effectively. Only men who are highly disciplined, fit and tough, self reliant and well led, can stand the test of fatigue and of severe enemy bombing and machine gunning under all conditions.

32. Ammunition

It is suggested that the War Office wastage scales provide a sound basis for estimating reserves for a large force on a long term basis and presupposes that at any one time only a portion of the force will be in action. For a small force actively engaged these scales are considered too small.

Layout of B.O.W. and B.O.D.

33. It is considered that wherever possible existing houses should be used for storage as opposed to building sheds. 1 and 3 sub-depots should be underground to avoid losses by bombing and fire.

34. It is suggested that the portions of the B.O.W. should be intermingled with the B.O.D. in proximity to the sub-depots for which they work.

Transport in Depots

35. The permanent allocation of a small amount of R.A.S.C. transport to R.A.O.C. Base depots would enable these depots to fulfil urgent demands rapidly.

Issues of stores at Docks direct to Units

36. To avoid incorrect issues it is considered most inadvisable for any items to be issued direct to units in the Docks. Stores should be taken to Depots where they can be checked and correct issues made. Direct issues will probably produce incorrect demands by the Service and provision figures will become confused.

APPENDIX B

ORDER OF BATTLE

FORCE HQ

Force HQ
Force sigs
42 Fd Coy RE less one sec
1 Welch
RE stores Depot
231 MT Coy RASC
Sup Depot RASC
Fd Bakery RASC
5 Ind Bde Workshops RAOC
Ordnance Depot RAOC
Amn Depot RAOC
1003 Docks Operating Coy
606 Palestine Pioneer Coy
1004)
1005)   Cypriot Pioneer Coys
1007)
1008)

HERAKLION SECTOR

HQ 14 Inf Bde and Sig Sec
2 BW
2 Y & L
2 Leicesters
2 A & SH with det at MESSARA PLAIN
7 Med Regt RA (armed as Inf)
2/4 Aust Inf BN
Det 3 H (6 lt tanks)
Det 7 RTR (5 lt tanks)
234 Med Bty RA (13 fd guns)
7 Aust Lt AA Bty less one tp and one sec (6 Bofors)
One tp 156 Lt AA Bty RA (4 Bofors)
Two secs C Hy AA Bty RM (four 3 inch guns)
One sec 23 Lt AA Bty RM (two 2 pr pom-poms)
One sec 15 Coast Regt RA (two 4 inch guns)
Sec 42 Fd Coy RE
Det 189 Fd Amb
3 Greek Regt (two bns)
7 Greek Regt (two bns)

RETIMO SECTOR

HQ 19 Aust Inf Bde and Sig Sec
2/1 Aust Inf Bn   At airdrome
2/7 Aust Inf Bn
2/8 Aust Inf Bn
2/11 Aust Inf Bn   At airdrome
One Aust MG Coy
Det 7 RTR (two I tanks)
Sec 106 RHA (two 2 pr A/Tk guns)
X Coast Bty (two 4 inch guns)
2/3 Fd Regt RAA (14 fd guns)
2/8 Fd Coy RAE
Two Greek Bns

Appendix B.....2

MALEME SECTOR

HQ NZ Div and Div Sigs
Det 3 H (10 lt tanks)
Det 7 RTR (two I tanks)
One lt Tp RA (four 3.7 hows)
One Sec Lt Arty RA (two 3.7 Hows)
27 Fd Bty NZA (ten 75 mm guns)
One tp and one sec 156 Lt AA Bty RA (6 Bofors)
One tp 7 Aust Lt AA Bty (4 Bofors)
One Sec C AA Bty Rm (two 3 inch guns)
Z Coast Bty RM (two 4 inch guns)
7 Fd Coy NZE)
5 Fd Park Coy NZE) employed as Inf
19 A Tps Coy NZE
4 NZ Inf Bde.   ) Force Reserve. <u>NOT</u>
  HQ and Bde Sig Sec) to be employed without
  18 Bn   ref to Force HQ
  19 Bn
  One MG Pl
5 NZ Inf Bde
  NQ and Bde Sig Sec
  21 Bn
  22 Bn
  23 Bn
  28 Bn
  Two MG Pls
10 NZ Inf Bde (improvised)
  HQ and Bde Sig Sec
  Composite Bn (NZA and NZASC)
  Div Cav Det
  20 Bn
  6 Greek Bn
  8 Greek Bn
  Two MG Pls less one sec
5 Fd Amb NZMC
6 Fd Amb NZMC

Appendix B.....3

SUDA BAY SECTOR

HQ MNBDO and Sigs (Sector Hq)
HQ 52 Lt AA Regt RA
151 Hy AA Bty RA (light 3.7 inch)
129 Lt AA Bty RA (12 Bofors)
156 Lt AA Bty RA (less two tps and one sec (2 Bofors)
One Sec 7 Aust Lt AA Bty (two Bofors)
23 Lt AA Bty RM less two tps (no guns)
HQ Hy AA Regt RM
A Hy AA Bty RM (eight 3 inch guns)
One Sec C Hy AA Bty RM (two 3 inch guns)
234 Hy AA Bty RA (eight 3.7 inch guns)
304 S/L Bty RA (20 lights)
5 S/L Bty RM (no lights)
Sec 106 RHA (two 2 pr A/Tk guns)

HQ 15 Coast Regt RA
   Z Coast Bty RA)   two 12 prs
   207 Coast Bty RA)   two 6 inch guns
   13 Notts Bty RA)   two 4 inch guns
   7 Notts Bty RA   )   two DELs
   One MG Pl NZ   )

1 Rangers
102 RHA (armed as inf)
106 RHA (armed as inf)
16 Aust Inf Bn (composite and improvised)
17 Aust Inf Bn ("   "   "   )
Perivolians Bn ("   "   "   )
2/2 Aust Fd Regt (armed as inf)
2/3 Aust Fd Regt ("   "   ")
2 Greek Bn
Base and harbor details
189 Fd Amb
1 Tented Hospital RN

www.ingramcontent.com/pod-product-compliance
Lightning Source LLC
Chambersburg PA
CBHW081848170426
43199CB00018B/2850